Be prepared...
To learn...
To succeed...

Get **REA**dy. It all starts here. REA's preparation for the ASK8 is **fully aligned** with New Jersey's Core Curriculum Content Standards.

READY, SET, GO!®

New Jersey
NJ ASK8
Language Arts Literacy

With REA's TestWare® on CD-ROM

Staff of Research & Education Association

Research & Education Association
Visit our website at
www.rea.com

Research & Education Association
61 Ethel Road West
Piscataway, New Jersey 08854
E-mail: info@rea.com

Ready, Set, Go!®
New Jersey ASK8–Eighth Grade
Language Arts Literacy
with TestWare® on CD-ROM

"Funnel Web" photo (p. 93) by Amit Kulkarni
"Sheet Web" photo (p. 93) by Alan Bauer

Printed in the United States of America

Library of Congress Control Number 2010936972

ISBN 13: 978-07386-0878-5
ISBN 10: 0-7386-0878-5

Table of Contents

ABOUT REA vii

ACKNOWLEDGMENTS vii

SUCCEEDING ON THE NJ ASK8 LANGUAGE ARTS viii
    About this Book and TestWare® viii
    How to Use this Book and TestWare® viii
    Why Students Are Required to Take the ASK8 x
    What's on the ASK8 x
    NJ ASK LAL Design: Grade 8 x
    ASK8 Language Arts Literacy Clusters xi
    Preparing for the Test xii
    Sound Advice for Test Day xiii
    Tips for Parents xiv

PRETEST 1

PRETEST ANSWERS 20

PART 1: READING   27

Lesson 1: Recognition of a Theme or Central Idea 27

Lesson 2: Paraphrasing/Retelling and
Making Tentative Predictions of Meaning 47

Lesson 3: Recognition of Text Organization
and Purpose for Reading, Extrapolation
of Information/Following Directions 64

Lesson 4: Making Judgments, Forming Opinions, and Drawing Conclusions 84

Lesson 5: Interpretation of Textual Conventions and Literary Elements 101

PART 2: WRITING, REVISING, AND VIEWING — 121

Lesson 1: Writing 122

Lesson 2: Writing to Speculate 136

Lesson 3: Writing to Analyze/Explain 140

Lesson 4: Writing to Persuade 143

POSTTEST 151

POSTTEST ANSWERS 178

APPENDIX 189

ANSWER SHEETS 211

Installing REA's TestWare® 240

About Research & Education Association

Founded in 1959, Research & Education Association is dedicated to publishing the finest and most effective educational materials—including software, study guides, and test preps—for students in middle school, high school, college, graduate school, and beyond.

Today, REA's wide-ranging catalog is a leading resource for teachers, students, and professionals.

We invite you to visit us at *www.rea.com* to find out how "REA is making the world smarter."

Acknowledgments

We would like to thank Larry B. Kling, Vice President, Editorial, for his editorial direction; Pam Weston, Publisher, for setting the quality standards for production integrity and managing the publication to completion; John Paul Cording, Vice President, Technology, for coordinating the design and development of REA's TestWare® software; Alice Leonard, Senior Editor, for project management; Diane Goldschmidt and Kathleen Casey, Senior Editors, for their editorial contributions; Heena Patel, Technology Project Manager, for software testing; Christine Saul, Senior Graphic Designer, for cover design; Jeremy Rech, Graphic Designer, for interior page design; and Caragraphics for typesetting the pages.

We most especially wish to thank Polly Taylor, eighth grade English Language Literacy teacher at Dwight D. Eisenhower Middle School, Berlin Township, N.J., for sharing her experience and insights with us for this new edition.

SUCCEEDING ON THE NJ ASK8 LANGUAGE ARTS LITERACY ASSESSMENT

ABOUT THIS BOOK AND TestWare®

This book, along with REA's exclusive TestWare® software, provides excellent preparation for the New Jersey ASK8 Language Arts Literacy Assessment. Inside you will find lessons, drills, strategies, and test practice—all of it with a single-minded focus: success on the NJ ASK8, an acronym that stands for Assessment of Skills and Knowledge.

We have also made every effort to make the book easy to read and navigate. The practice tests are included in two formats: in this book and on CD.

The book is divided into several parts. The first section is a **PRETEST**, which is half the length of an actual ASK8 test and introduces students to some of the key sections on the actual test:

- Explanatory writing prompt
- Informational reading passage
- Narrative reading passage
- Persuasive writing prompt

We recommend that you begin your preparation by first taking the practice exams on your computer. The software provides timed conditions and instantaneous, accurate scoring that makes it easier to pinpoint your strengths and weaknesses.

Following the pretest are **two lesson sections:**

Part 1 teaches students about the different types of ASK8 questions and skills on the reading portion of the test;

Part 2 instructs students on the writing, revising, and viewing portions of the test;

Finally, a full-length **POSTTEST** appears at the end of the book and on the TestWare® CD.

At this time, speaking, listening, and viewing are not part of the NJ ASK 8 LAL test. The classroom teacher assesses these skills. However, because these skills are vital to a full curriculum, we provide a special supplementary section on them to be used where needed by the student.

HOW TO USE THIS BOOK AND TestWare®

FOR STUDENTS: To make getting through the book as easy as possible, we've included icons shown on the next page that highlight sections like lessons, questions, and answers. You'll find that our practice tests are very much like the actual ASK8 you'll encounter on test day. The best way to prepare for a test is to read over the test information and study tips. Take the pretest on CD-ROM to determine your strengths and weaknesses, and then study the course review material, focusing on your specific problem areas. The course review includes the information you need to know when taking the test. Make sure to follow up your diagnostic work by taking the Posttest on CD-ROM to become familiar with the format and feel of the NJ ASK8 Language Arts Literacy Assessment.

FOR PARENTS: New Jersey has created grade-appropriate standards for English language arts and has listed them in clusters, which are explained below. Students need to meet these standards as measured by the ASK8. Our book will help your child review the ASK8 and prepare for the Language Arts Literacy exam. It includes review sections, drills, and two practice tests complete with explanations to help your child focus on the areas he or she needs to work on to help master the test.

FOR TEACHERS: No doubt, you are already familiar with the ASK8 and its format. Begin by assigning students the pretest. An answer key and detailed explanations follow the pretest. Then work through each of the lessons in succession. When students have completed the subject review, they should move on to the posttest. Answers and answer explanations follow the posttest.

Icons Explained

Icons make navigating through the book easier by highlighting sections like lessons, questions, and answers as explained below:

 Question

 Answer

 Tip

 Lesson

 Activity

 Writing Task

WHY STUDENTS ARE REQUIRED TO TAKE THE ASK8

In 1996 the New Jersey State Board of Education adopted Core Curriculum Content Standards that define New Jersey's expectations for student learning. The board updated the Language Arts Literacy standards in 2004, 2007, and again in 2009. The latest version of the Common Core State Standards was adopted as of June 20, 2010. To determine how well a student is advancing and whether the student is on course to perform well in high school, eighth grade students are required to take the ASK8.

It is one of the key tools used to identify students who need additional instruction to master the knowledge and skills detailed in the Core Curriculum, the standards that guide education in New Jersey.

WHAT'S ON THE ASK8

The NJ ASK is composed of a reading section and a writing section. The reading cluster of the test has students read four passages that are either narrative or informational in content. They then respond to related multiple-choice questions and constructed- response items.

The writing section contains one persuasive prompt and either one explanatory prompt or one speculative prompt. The persuasive prompt asks for the student's point of view or opinion about a given controversy. The explanatory and speculative prompts present students with a springboard topic from which to write a composition.

NJ ASK LAL Design: Grade 8

Text Types/Strand (additional field test content embedded throughout)	Reading Selections	Multiple-Choice (number of items)	Open-Ended (number of items)	Writing Tasks (number of items)	Time on Task(s) (in minutes)	Total Points
Writing: Persuasive Prompt				1	45 minutes each	12
Writing: Explanatory or Speculative Prompt				1	30 minutes each	6
Reading passages	4	36	4		30 minutes each	52
Total				2	195 minutes	70

Timing does not include time for distributing and collecting materials, reading directions, and giving breaks to children.

Approximate testing times:

Language Arts Literacy, Day 1	1 hour, 45 minutes
Language Arts Literacy, Day 2	2 hours, 15 minutes

All questions are based on ASK8 language arts literacy content clusters and skills, which are given in the table on the following pages.

ASK8 Language Arts Literacy Clusters

Cluster 1: Reading (Standard 3.1)

	Page Numbers
Recognize a theme or central idea	27, 28, 31, 35, 37, 38, 40, 45, 46, 98. 105, 109,110, 113, 114, 115
Recognize details that develop or support the main idea	29, 31, 32, 36, 40, 41, 46, 90, 91, 94, 98,109, 105, 113
Extrapolate information and/or follow directions	36, 40, 41, 52, 53, 54, 58, 61, 62, 65, 68, 69, 77, 76, 81, 82, 119
Paraphrase, retell, or interpret words, phrases, or sentences from the text	47, 61, 78, 90, 100, 115, 118
Recognize the organization and structure of the text	64, 68, 76
Recognize a purpose for reading	45, 64, 69, 72, 73, 82, 83, 99
Make tentative predictions of meaning	47, 56, 57, 72, 114
Make judgments, form opinions, and draw conclusions from the text	62, 63, 68, 71, 77, 78, 84, 85, 87, 88, 94, 106
Interpret textual conventions and literary elements	102, 105, 109, 114, 119, 120

Cluster 2: Writing (Standard 3.2)

	Page Numbers
Respond clearly and appropriately to a given prompt	121, 122, 132, 135, 136, 142, 145
Select a focus and appropriate details to support it	122, 123, 127, 132, 136, 139, 140, 142, 143, 145
Organize the response to include an introduction, appropriate transitions, and a conclusion	122, 124, 127, 128, 129, 132, 134, 136, 137, 139, 140, 142, 143, 145, 148
Use elaboration to engage the audience	122, 127, 136
Use varied sentence structure and word choice	122, 129, 132, 134, 140, 142
Use conventions of print and literary forms	126, 132, 136, 140
Use language appropriate to the audience	122, 127, 129, 136, 139, 140, 142, 143, 145, 148, 150
Revise and edit a passage for content/organization, usage, sentence construction, and mechanics	124, 127, 129, 132, 134, 136, 140, 142, 145, 148
Synthesize information from a variety of sources in a written response	136, 140, 142, 143

TIPS FOR THE STUDENT

There are plenty of things students can do before and during the actual test to improve their test-taking performance. The good thing is that most of the tips described below are easy!

Preparing for the Test

Test Anxiety

Do you get nervous when your teacher talks about taking a test? A certain amount of anxiety is normal, and it actually may help you prepare better for the test by getting you motivated. Nonetheless, too much anxiety is a bad thing and may keep you from properly focusing. Here are some things to consider that may help relieve test anxiety:

- Share how you are feeling with your parents and your teachers. They may have ways of helping you deal with your concerns.

- Keep on top of your game. Are you behind in your homework and class assignments? A lot of your classwork-related anxiety and stress will simply go away if you keep up with your homework assignments and classwork. And then you can focus on the test with a clearer mind.

- Relax. Take a deep breath or two. You should do this especially if you get anxious while taking the test.

Study Tips and Taking the Test

- **Learn the test's format.** Don't be surprised. By taking a practice test ahead of time you'll know what the test looks like, how much time you will have, how many questions there are, and what kinds of questions are going to appear on the actual exam. Knowing ahead of time is much better than being surprised.

- **Read the entire question.** Pay attention to what kind of answer a question or word problem is looking for. Reread the question if it does not make sense to you, and try to note the parts of the question needed for figuring out the right answer.

- **Read all the answers.** On a multiple-choice test, the last answer could also be the right answer. You won't know unless you read all the possible answers to a question.

- **It's not a guessing game.** If you don't know the answer to a question, don't make an uneducated guess. And don't randomly pick just any answer, either. As you read over each possible answer to a question, note any answers that are obviously wrong, then select one of the remaining answers. Each obviously wrong answer you identify and eliminate greatly improves your chances at selecting the right answer.

- **Don't get stuck on questions.** Don't spend too much time on any one question. Doing this takes away time from the other questions. Work on the easier questions first. Skip the really hard questions and come back to them if there is still enough time.

- **Accuracy counts.** Make sure you record your answer in the correct space on your answer sheet. Fixing mistakes later wastes valuable time.

- **Finished early?** Use this time wisely and double-check your answers.

SOUND ADVICE FOR TEST DAY

The night before. Getting a good night's rest keeps your mind sharp and focused for the test.

The morning of the test. Have a good breakfast. Dress in comfortable clothes. Keep in mind that you don't want to be too hot or too cold while taking the test. Get to school on time. Give yourself time to gather your thoughts and calm down before the test begins.

Three Steps for Taking the Test

1. **READ.** Read the entire question and then read all the possible answers.

2. **ANSWER.** Answer the easier questions first and then go back to the more difficult questions.

3. **DOUBLE-CHECK.** Go back and check your work if time permits.

TIPS FOR PARENTS

- Encourage your child to take responsibility for homework and class assignments. Help your child create a study schedule. Mark the test's date on a family calendar as a reminder for both of you.

- Talk to your child's teachers. Ask them for progress reports on an ongoing basis.

- Commend your child's study and test successes. Praise your child for successfully following a study schedule, for doing homework, and for any work done well.

- Attack test anxiety head-on. Your child may experience nervousness or anxiety about the test. You may even be anxious, too. Here are some helpful tips on dealing with a child's test anxiety:

  - Talk about the test openly and positively with your child. An ongoing dialogue can not only relieve your child's anxieties but also serve as a progress report of how your child feels about the test. When talking together, make sure your child understands what areas he or she is going to be tested on.

  - Form realistic expectations of your child's testing abilities.

  - Be a "test cheerleader." Your encouragement to do his or her best on the test can alleviate your child's test anxiety.

  - Have your child use the last days before the test to review all tested subject areas.

PRETEST

This test is also on CD-ROM in our special interactive NJ ASK8 Language Arts Literacy TestWare®. It is highly recommended that you first take this exam on computer. You will then have the additional study features and benefits of enforced timed conditions and instant, accurate scoring. See page viii for guidance on how to get the most out of our NJ ASK8 Language Arts Literacy software.

PART 1:
EXPLANATORY WRITING TASK

For this part of your test, you will be asked to respond to an explanatory writing prompt. You will have 30 minutes for this part of the test. Plan and draft your answer on a separate piece of paper. Revise and edit your draft. Then copy your final response into this book. If you finish ahead of time, do not go on to the next part of the test. Wait for your teacher to continue.

My November Guest
by Robert Frost

My sorrow, when she's here with me,
 Thinks these dark days of autumn rain
Are beautiful as days can be;
She loves the bare, the withered tree;
 She walks the sodden pasture lane.

Her pleasure will not let me stay.
 She talks and I am fain to list:
She's glad the birds are gone away,
She's glad her simple worsted gray
 Is silver now with clinging mist.

The desolate, deserted trees,
 The faded earth, the heavy sky,
The beauties she so truly sees,
She thinks I have no eye for these,
 And vexes me for reason why.

Not yesterday I learned to know
 The love of bare November days
Before the coming of the snow,
But it were vain to tell her so,
 And they are better for her praise.

WRITING TASK A

In this poem, the reader learns about the hidden beauties of a cold November day.

- What is your favorite month or season of the year?
- If you were asked to write a poem, song, or story about your favorite month or season what characteristics and aspects of the month/season would you include in your writing?

PREWRITING/PLANNING SPACE

When you finish your planning, copy your final response on the lined pages in the answer sheet section at the back of this book.

END OF PART 1
Be sure to write your draft on the lined pages
in the answer sheet section at the back of this
book. You may check your work on this part only.
DO NOT GO ON TO THE NEXT PAGE

STOP

PRETEST: PART 2
READING: INFORMATIONAL

In this part of the test, you will read an informational passage and then respond to the multiple-choice and open-ended questions that follow it. You will have 30 minutes for this part of the test. You may look back at the passage and make notes in your test booklet if you like, but you must write your answers on the answer sheet.

Introduction: This article is about a man who made an amazing discovery.

Digging Up James Fort

Archaeologist William Kelso had a shovel, a wheelbarrow, and a mission. He was determined to unearth the remains of James Fort, an early British settlement in America. Most archaeologists thought he would discover nothing but dirt. They believed that over the centuries the James River had washed away the land on which the fort had once stood. Kelso was in the minority who thought the fort, which he thought of as "an archaeological time capsule," could still be found.

Kelso received permission to begin an excavation on the 22-acre island in Virginia where the fort had been constructed in 1607. He commenced digging with his simple tools as local people gathered to observe him. Within hours, Kelso had found more evidence than he'd anticipated. He found metal buttons, armor and weapons, pieces of copper, animal bones, and fragments of dishes, pots, and pipes. Kelso had located a trash pit—an early kind of dump—of enormous proportions.

When he showed historians what he had found, they were astounded. A group of historians decided to give Kelso funding to continue his excavation. With that money, Kelso was able to hire a team of assistants and purchase better equipment. They found more than four hundred thousand

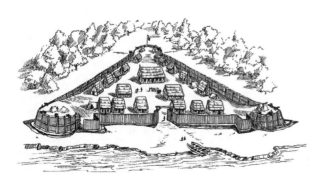

artifacts from the colonial years. One of their most important discoveries was not an artifact at all. In fact, to the untrained eye, this discovery looked just like black ink stains on the dirt. But Kelso knew that these stains represented the remains of the wooden walls of the fort. The team knew then that they hadn't just been digging in a nameless old dump. They had actually found the outline of two of James Fort's three walls, totaling two-hundred-and-fifty feet of logs. After uncovering the whole area between the walls, Kelso realized he had located the spot where the American government was first **conceived**, hundreds of years previously. He was soon to discover evidence, however, that that was not all that happened in James Fort.

The history of James Fort, and the whole area called Jamestown, is a terrible one. Only about one out of six people who moved there from England survived. The colony was characterized by power struggles, massacres, and starvation. Many historians believed that poor planning was the cause of these problems. When British leaders decided to colonize Jamestown, they did not carefully consider what type of citizens should immigrate there. Instead, they mostly sent aristocrats, servants, and craftspeople. Few of these people knew how to grow their own food. The aristocrats were considered lazy and selfish and spent their time arguing over who should be in control of the colony. Furthermore, the British leaders who organized the colony were mostly concerned with finding gold. They encouraged the colonists to search for gold and barter with the Native Americans. "The colony's primary goal was to make a profit for the sponsors," Kelso wrote. This greedy

GO ON TO THE NEXT PAGE. ➡

goal left the colonists little time to improve their own community.

Kelso's discoveries contradicted some popular beliefs about what had happened in Jamestown. He discovered that the people of James Fort were not lazy. They had many tools that they used for their everyday tasks. Scattered around the fort and the trash pits were bullet molds, metal-working tools, glass-making tools, animal bones, weapons, fishhooks, and oyster shells. Researchers concluded that the colonists had hunted, fished, and made useful crafts.

Kelso's team also found lots of metal, especially copper, at the site. In the 1600s, the British had hoped that Native Americans would be impressed with metal tools and ornaments, since most Native Americans relied on tools made of stone and wood. The Jamestown colonists expected to be able to trade copper to the natives for food and gold. However, some British sailors secretly sold copper directly to the Native Americans in the area. Because of this, the natives didn't need any more copper and didn't want to trade with the colonists. This was one of the primary factors in the downfall of James Fort.

The colonists continually struggled to find enough food. At first they relied on gifts of corn from nearby Native American villages. However, a severe drought caused most crops to die, and food became scarce all over Virginia; they called this "the starving time." The Native Americans could no longer afford to give food away. The Jamestown colonists were starving and desperate. They began attacking native villages in order to steal food. The natives in turn attacked the colonists and surrounded James Fort. Trapped inside their fort, hundreds of colonists died of starvation and disease. Kelso's team found a hastily made cemetery full of Jamestown's most unfortunate residents.

The early years of Jamestown were a tragic failure, but they gave many people hopes for new opportunities in America. Jamestown went on to become the first capital of Virginia. Soldiers camped there in the Revolutionary and Civil Wars. Thousands of new colonists immigrated to the area to begin new lives, having learned valuable lessons from the hardships that had taken place in James Fort.

1. The excavation was unusual because it

   A. took place on an island.
   B. was authorized by the government.
   C. involved digging deep into the ground.
   D. was started by a single dedicated person.

2. In paragraph 3, the word <u>astounded</u> means

   A. surprised.
   B. angry.
   C. unconvinced.
   D. jealous.

3. Which sentence best supports the idea that Kelso's discoveries differed from some popular beliefs about what had happened in Jamestown?

   A. "They'd actually found the outline of James Fort."
   B. "However, a severe drought caused most crops to die."
   C. "The Jamestown colonists were starving and desperate."
   D. "He found out that the people of James Fort were not lazy."

4. What was Kelso's most important discovery at Jamestown?

   A. fishhooks
   B. animal bones
   C. working tools
   D. wooden walls

5. The author most likely wrote this article

   A. to inform.
   B. to entertain.
   C. to persuade.
   D. to provide instructions.

6. This article would be most helpful when

   A. reporting about Native American settlements.
   B. writing a report about the history of archaeology.
   C. preparing a presentation on recently discovered facts about American historical sites.
   D. learning about the class system of the colonies.

GO ON TO THE NEXT PAGE. ➡

7. Which word below is an antonym for the word <u>commenced</u>?

   A. began
   B. delayed
   C. hurried
   D. ended

8. Use the glossary entry below to answer the question that follows.

   Glossary:

   conceived (verb)—
   1. imagined or thought of something
   2. devised, created, or invented something
   3. became pregnant
   4. understood

   Which entry provides the best definition for the word <u>conceived</u> as it is used in paragraph 3?

   A. Entry #2
   B. Entry #1
   C. Entry #4
   D. Entry #3

9. Which fact from the article could easily be represented in a chart?

   A. Only about one out of six people that moved to James Fort from England survived.
   B. It has been over 400 years since the fort was constructed in Virginia.
   C. About 30 percent of the citizens of Jamestown were aristocrats.
   D. None of these facts as represented are included in the article.

DIRECTIONS FOR QUESTION 10: Write your response in the space provided in the answer sheet section of this book.

10. William Kelso studied his findings to learn about the history of Jamestown. Explain TWO ways in which he used his findings. Use information from the article to support your answer.

DIRECTIONS FOR QUESTION 11: Write your response in the space provided in the answer sheet section of this book.

11. A time capsule is something that shows future generations what life was like during that moment in history. In modern times, people have created time capsules on purpose by burying ordinary items or messages in locked containers. In paragraph 1, what does the author mean when he writes that William Kelso thought of James Fort as "an archaeological time capsule"?

   Use information from the article to support your response.

END OF PART 2
You may check your work on this part only.
DO NOT GO ON TO THE NEXT PAGE

STOP

PRETEST: PART 3
READING: NARRATIVE

In this part of the test, you will read a narrative passage and then respond to the multiple-choice and open-ended questions that follow it. You will have 30 minutes for this part of the test. You may look back at the passage and make notes in your test booklet if you like, but you must write your answers on the answer sheet.

INTRODUCTION: In this excerpt from the novel The Secret Garden, *Mary and her friend Dickon consider taking Colin, an injured boy who also seems to be paralyzed, to see a garden that they consider to be their secret place.*

The Secret Garden
by Frances Hodgson Burnett
(from Chapter 15 – "Nest Building")

There was every joy on earth in the secret garden that morning, and in the midst of them came a delight more delightful than all, because it was more wonderful. Swiftly something flew across the wall and darted through the trees to a close grown corner, a little flare of red-breasted bird with something hanging from its beak. Dickon stood quite still and put his hand on Mary almost as if they had suddenly found themselves laughing in a church.

"We munnot stir," he whispered in broad Yorkshire. "We munnot scarce breathe. I knowed he was mate-huntin' when I seed him last. It's Ben Weatherstaff's robin. He's buildin' his nest. He'll stay here if us don't fight him." They settled down softly upon the grass and sat there without moving.

"Us mustn't seem as if us was watchin' him too close," said Dickon. "He'd be out with us for good if he got th' notion us was interferin' now. . . . They've got their way o' thinkin' and doin' things an' a body had better not meddle. You can lose a friend in springtime easier than any other season if you're too curious."

"If we talk about him I can't help looking at him," Mary said as softly as possible. "We must talk of something else. There is something I want to tell you."

"He'll like it better if us talks o' somethin' else," said Dickon. "What is it tha's got to tell me?"

"Well–do you know about Colin?" she whispered.

He turned his head to look at her.

"What does tha' know about him?" he asked.

"I've seen him. I have been to talk to him every day this week. He wants me to come. He says I'm making him forget about being ill and dying," answered Mary.

Dickon looked actually relieved as soon as the surprise died away from his round face. . . .

10

***

"Colin's so afraid of it himself that he won't sit up," said Mary. "He says he's always thinking that if he should feel a lump coming he should go crazy and scream himself to death."

"Eh! he oughtn't to lie there thinkin' things like that," said Dickon. "No lad could get well as thought them sort o' things."

The fox was lying on the grass close by him, looking up to ask for a pat now and then, and Dickon bent down and rubbed his neck softly and thought a few minutes in silence. Presently he lifted his head and looked round the garden.

"When first we got in here," he said, "it seemed like everything was gray. Look round now and tell me if tha' doesn't see a difference."

Mary looked and caught her breath a little.

GO ON TO THE NEXT PAGE. ➡

16 "Why!" she cried, "the gray wall is changing. It is as if a green mist were creeping over it. It's almost like a green gauze veil."

"Aye," said Dickon. "An' it'll be greener and greener till th' gray's all gone. Can tha' guess what I was thinkin'?"

"I know it was something nice," said Mary eagerly. "I believe it was something about Colin."

"I was thinkin' that if he was out here he wouldn't be watchin' for lumps to grow on his back; he'd be watchin' for buds to break on th' rose-bushes, an' he'd likely be healthier," explained Dickon. "I was wonderin' if us could ever get him in th' humor to come out here an' lie under th' trees in his carriage."

"I've been wondering that myself. I've thought of it almost every time I've talked to him," said Mary. "I've wondered if he could keep a secret and I've wondered if we could bring him here without any one seeing us. I thought perhaps you could push his carriage. The doctor said he must have fresh air and if he wants us to take him out no one dare disobey him. He won't go out for other people and perhaps they will be glad if he will go out with us. He could order the gardeners to keep away so they wouldn't find out."

Dickon was thinking very hard as he scratched Captain's back.

"It'd be good for him, I'll warrant," he said. "Us'd not be thinkin' he'd better never been born. Us'd be just two children watchin' a garden grow, an' he'd be another. Two lads an' a little lass just lookin' on at th' springtime. I warrant it'd be better than doctor's stuff."

"He's been lying in his room so long and he's always been so afraid of his back that it has made him queer," said Mary. "He knows a good many things out of books but he doesn't know anything else. He says he has been too ill to notice things and he hates going out of doors and hates gardens and gardeners. But he likes to hear about this garden because it is a secret. I daren't tell him much but he said he wanted to see it."

"Us'll have him out here sometime for sure," said Dickon. "I could push his carriage well enough. Has tha' noticed how th' robin an' his mate has been workin' while we've been sittin' here? Look at him perched on that branch wonderin' where it'd be best to put that twig he's got in his beak."

He made one of his low whistling calls and the robin turned his head and looked at him inquiringly, still holding his twig. . . .

"Tha' knows us won't trouble thee," he said to the robin. "Us is near bein' wild things ourselves. Us is nest-buildin' too, bless thee. Look out tha' doesn't tell on us."

And though the robin did not answer, because his beak was occupied, Mary knew that when he flew away with his twig to his own corner of the garden the darkness of his dew-bright eye meant that he would not tell their secret for the world.

GO ON TO THE NEXT PAGE. ➡

12. Why doesn't Mary tell Colin about the secret garden at first?

   A. She is not sure she can trust him.

   B. She is not sure he is well enough.

   C. She does not think he will like Dickon.

   D. She does not know if he wants to see it.

13. Which of the following contributes MOST to Dickon's unusual character?

   A. He speaks with a difficult accent.

   B. He is excited about meeting Colin.

   C. He communicates with wild animals.

   D. He likes to spend time in the secret garden.

14. At the end of the passage, which BEST describes the narrator's tone?

   A. suspenseful

   B. mysterious

   C. playful

   D. humorous

15. In paragraph 10, what does the author mean when she writes that "Dickon looked actually relieved"?

   A. He was happy because Ben told him that he and Mary could work in the garden.

   B. He was happy because he no longer had to keep the secret about Colin.

   C. He was happy because Mary stopped looking at the robin building its nest.

   D. He was happy because Colin knew the location of the secret garden.

16. At what point in the story does Mary decide to tell Dickon that she knows about Colin?

   A. When Dickon tells her that he already knows about Colin.

   B. When she sees Dickon sitting still and quiet in the garden.

   C. When he says they must ignore the robin building his nest.

   D. When Mary sees a robin flying across the wall and into the trees.

GO ON TO THE NEXT PAGE. ➡

17. In paragraph 16, the creeping green mist is compared to a green gauze veil using a _____.

    A. simile
    B. metaphor
    C. hyperbole
    D. onomatopoeia

18. Which word below is a synonym for the word queer in paragraph 23?

    A. happy
    B. strange
    C. sleepy
    D. healthy

19. The author probably wrote this story

    A. to inform.
    B. to entertain.
    C. to persuade.
    D. to provide instructions.

20. This chapter excerpt would be most useful when

    A. providing examples of dialect in dialogue.
    B. presenting information about gardens.
    C. teaching others how to act around animals.
    D. explaining why some things should be kept secret.

21. Based on the clues in the story, how do the children feel about the animals in the garden?

    A. The children don't like the animals and want to keep them out of the garden.
    B. The children respect the animals and don't want to disturb them in the garden.
    C. The children think the animals are going to ruin their secret.
    D. The children are jealous of the animals and want to trade places with them.

GO ON TO THE NEXT PAGE. ➡

22. How does the setting change as Mary and Dickon talk about Colin?

    A.   Clouds roll in and the sun disappears.

    B.   It gets really cold in the garden.

    C.   The gray color of the garden starts to turn green.

    D.   Flowers start to bloom in every corner of the garden.

23. What is the issue that Mary and Dickon are discussing and how is it resolved?

    A.   Mary and Dickon talk about how to help the robin build its nest. They decide to pile up twigs.

    B.   Mary and Dickon talk about how to keep the garden secret. They decide to hide the entrance.

    C.   Mary and Dickon talk about whether or not they should share the secret garden with their sick friend Colin. They decide that they would find a way to bring him there.

    D.   Mary and Dickon talk about whether or not Mary's father would let him keep the fox as a pet. When they ask about the fox, Mary's father doesn't allow Mary to keep it.

24. In paragraph 16, what does the phrase "green gauze veil" mean?

    A.   A green mist is partially hiding the wall.

    B.   The wall is covered with a soft green fabric.

    C.   A green mist is creeping into the secret garden.

    D.   Young green leaves are growing on the wall.

25. Which of the following phrases best describes the theme of this passage?

    A.   Keeping secrets can be difficult.

    B.   Wild animals make good companions.

    C.   We should always help our friends.

    D.   Nature has the power to heal.

GO ON TO THE NEXT PAGE. ➡

DIRECTIONS FOR QUESTION 26: Write your response in the space provided in the answer sheet section of this book.

26. Throughout the story, Mary and Dickon do not want others to learn about the secret garden. If you were Mary or Dickon

- would you tell others about the secret garden?

- why or why not?

Use information from the story to support your answer.

DIRECTIONS FOR QUESTION 27: Write your response in the space provided in the answer sheet section of this book.

27. At the end of the story, Mary and Dickon discuss taking Colin to the garden.

- Why do they think that this is a good idea?

- Give TWO or more other reasons why they should take Colin to see the garden.

<u>END OF PART 3</u>
Be sure to write your draft on the lined pages in the answer sheet section at the back of this book. You may check your work on this part only.

PERSUASIVE WRITING TASK
PART 4

For this part of your test, you will be asked to respond to a writing prompt. You will have 45 minutes to complete this writing task. Plan and draft your answer on a separate piece of paper. Revise and edit your draft. Then copy your final response into the answer sheets provided. If you finish ahead of time, do not go on to the next part of the test. Wait for your teacher to continue.

WRITING SITUATION

This year, two of your school's teachers have retired. To save money to build a new gymnasium, your principal has decided to offer instruction for several classes using distance education, meaning you would only "see" your teacher via a television screen when a video tape is played. When you complete assignments or take tests for these classes, the school secretary will email them to your teacher, who will grade them and mail them back.

PERSUASIVE WRITING TASK B

Write a letter to the editor of your school newspaper. Explain your views on the principal's decision requiring some classes to be taught using distance education. Use examples, facts, and other evidence to support your point of view.

GO ON TO THE NEXT PAGE. ➡

PREWRITING/PLANNING SPACE

When you finish your planning, copy your final response on the lined pages in the answer sheet section of this book.

END OF PART 4
Be sure to write your draft on the lined pages
in the answer sheet section at the back of this
book. You may check your work on this part only.

ASK8 Pretest Answer Key

Part 1

Sample answer: *The crisp leaves along the trail, the smell of earth and harvest, and the cool air are some of my favorite parts of the best season—fall! Autumn is the best time of year for so many reasons that I could probably write a whole album full of songs—an entire book full of poems about it. Most of those poems or songs would be about my three favorite things about autumn: Thanksgiving, Halloween, and the colors of the leaves.*

The best thing about fall is Thanksgiving. Visiting the local farms to get fresh veggies from the harvest, decorating the table, cooking the food, and visiting with family form some of my warmest memories of the season. Just the thought of the smell of fresh pumpkin pie, cranberry sauce, gravy, mashed potatoes, corn and all the trimmings makes my mouth water. Another great part about Thanksgiving is that there is always food leftover for the next few days.

Another one of my favorite things about fall is Halloween. Besides the candy and costumes, I really love to decorate pumpkins. My family gets all different shapes, sizes and colors of pumpkins and we create all different faces and designs. When we're done, we line them up along our path and put candles in them. When the kids come up for trick-or-treating, it looks really spooky.

I saved the most beautiful part of the season for last. The colors of the leaves—aren't they breathtaking? As soon as I notice that the leaves are changing, I ask my dad to take me for a long ride through the woods. The best road for this is a windy, hilly road so you can see the trees from different angles. I think my dad enjoys these rides just as much as me.

Although I like to see the lovely things earth has to offer throughout all her seasons, fall is my personal favorite. I could go on and on about all its wonderful features for hours and hours. Hopefully I have revived your love of the fall season. See you at the dinner table . . . gobble gobble!

Explanation: *The response stays focused on the prompt, appropriately addresses the audience, follows a single format, and is well organized. There are strong statements in the opening and closing that guide and inform the reader. The writing flows from one idea to the next and there are supportive details to support each main idea. There are some compositional risks, like the use of ellipsis (. . .) but the grammar, mechanics, and punctuation are otherwise accurate.*

Part 2

1. **D.** Recognizing supporting details (G16)

   The author makes a point of showing how the James Fort excavation was unusual because it was initiated, or begun, by a single dedicated archaeologist. The opening of the article describes how William Kelso worked alone in the beginning of his impressive task.

2. **A.** Paraphrasing/retelling (F1)

Look at the sentences before and after the sentence that uses the word <u>astounded</u> to help determine the meaning. You might think the others were angry, jealous, or unconvinced. However, note that after hearing about Kelso's discovery a group of historians decided to give him money to continue his work. William Kelso was the only person who expected to find something buried at James Fort; everyone else was surprised. Therefore, answer choice A is the correct answer.

3. **D.** Extrapolating information (G21)

The article explains that many historians believed that the tragedies at the Jamestown colony were caused by lazy colonists. However, by excavating the James Fort and finding evidence of hard work, Kelso proved that the colonists had not been lazy as believed.

4. **D.** Recognizing supporting details (G20)

The article says that finding the remains of the wooden fort was the most important discovery.

5. **A.** Recognizing author's purpose (G10, G20)

The content of the article provides facts and information. The passage was not written to entertain like a story would, does not provide instructions, and does not contain biased or persuasive language. The characteristics of the writing show that it was written to inform the reader.

6. **C.** Extrapolating information (G21)

Since this article focuses on new findings at one particular historical American site, it would be best used when presenting on this topic. Since it does not focus on a Native American settlement, answer A is incorrect. The article would not provide enough information to report on the history of archaeology, answer B. Finally, since the article contained little specific information about the class system, answer D is incorrect as well.

7. **D.** Understanding use of literary devices (G5)

An antonym is a word with the opposite meaning as the chosen word. Since *commenced* means *began*, the opposite definition would be *ended*, choice D.

8. **A.** Clarify word meanings (F5)

After reviewing the glossary definitions and the answer choices, the only term/definition that makes sense in the passage is *created* (definition #2).

9. **A.** Using organizational structures (A1)

The only answer that provides exact information that could be charted is answer A. The other choices only offer approximations of the data presented.

10. Drawing conclusions (G20, G21)

Sample answer: *The artifacts William Kelso found revealed the way people lived in Jamestown in the early 1600s. Objects like fishhooks and animal bones suggested that the people hunted and fished. Tools for making glass and metal showed that the people made useful crafts. Kelso also learned from things that weren't artifacts, like the stains left in the dirt by the fort's walls.*

11. Making tentative predictions of meaning (G8, G20)

Sample answer: *When William Kelso called James Fort an archaeological time capsule, he meant that the things he would find there could communicate information about the people who settled at Jamestown in 1607. Although the settlers did not purposely create a time capsule, Kelso and his team found evidence about their daily lives, including metal buttons, armor and weapons, tools, animal bones, and cemeteries, under the mounds of dirt near the James River.*

Part 3 Narrative

12. **A.** Recognizing supporting details (G20)

Mary says she has often considered telling Colin about the garden, but she is not yet sure if he can keep a secret. Therefore, answer choice A is the correct answer.

13. **C.** Making judgments (G20, G21)

This question asks you to identify the most unusual thing about Dickon. Dickon is petting a baby fox throughout the story and a crow perches on his shoulder. He also talks to a robin. His actions with animals contribute most to this unusual character. Therefore, answer choice C is the best answer.

14. **C.** Interpreting textual conventions and literary elements (G16)

The end of the story describes Dickon talking to the robin and says that Mary believes the robin will keep their secret. It is not particularly suspenseful, mysterious, or humorous. It is playful, so answer choice C is correct.

15. **B.** Making predictions (G8, G20)

To answer this question correctly, you need to read the paragraphs that come just before paragraph 10 and consider what Dickon has been discussing with Mary. She has just asked him if he knows about Colin. Dickon is obviously surprised to learn how much Mary knows about Colin. Answer choice B is the best answer.

16. **C.** Recognizing supporting details (G20)

Mary only tells Dickon that she knows about Colin when Dickon tells her they must talk about something other than the robin. Therefore, answer choice C is correct.

17. **A.** Understanding of literary devices (G5)

Similes are comparisons that are made using the words *like* or *as*. This comparison uses the word *like* to compare the green mist to a green gauze veil.

18. **B.** Understanding of literary devices (G5)

An antonym is a word with a similar meaning as the chosen word. Since *queer* means *weird* or *strange* in this sentence, the answer choice is B.

19. B. Understanding of text features (G)

This passage has many qualities of an entertaining story—characters, dialogue, specific setting, and conflict. The passage does not contain specific factual information, biased or persuasive language, or instructions.

20. A. Identifying literary techniques (G16)

The dialect used in this passage is quite unique. This passage is an example of how authors use dialect in dialogue to enrich the depiction of their characters. Although the topics of the other answer choices may be contained in the story, the passage wouldn't really serve as examples of them.

21. B. Comprehension skills (G)

In the beginning of the passage, the children do not want to disturb the robin that is building a nest. Another clue lies in Dickon's interaction with the fox. Finally, the children refer to the robin with respect again at the end of the story.

22. C. Comprehension skills (G)

While Mary and Dickon discuss Colin, they notice that the gray wall is turning green and the garden is getting greener.

23. C. Revising text predictions (E9)

The only topics the children discussed was whether or not Colin should visit the garden and how to get him out there without ruining their secret place.

24. D. Interpreting words, phrases, or sentences (F1)

Look at the passage carefully. There is no real mist; there is no real veil. The author is using imagery to create a picture in your mind. What is green in a garden? Leaves. Therefore, answer choice D is correct.

25. **D.** Recognizing a theme or central idea (E1)

Throughout this passage, the author uses images of nature to show the joyful effect on Mary and Dickon. At the end, Dickon states that perhaps being in the garden will be better medicine for Colin than "doctor's stuff." Therefore, answer choice D is the best answer.

26. Making predictions (G8, G20)

Sample answer: *If I were Mary or Dickon, I would not tell others about the secret garden. If they tell people how beautiful it is there, others will come to see it. Dickon has befriended many animals in the garden that might be scared off by newcomers. Telling others about the garden will only alter its beauty.*

27. Forming opinions (G8, G20)

Sample answer: *Mary and Dickon think it is a good idea to take Colin to the secret garden because Colin stays inside all of the time thinking about his illness. They think that the fresh air will do him good and that going out will keep him from thinking about how sick he is. In addition to these reasons, going to the garden might actually force Colin to make some friends and have some fun, which he seems to really need. It might make him appreciate the world around him and will improve his spirits.*

Part 4—Writing Task B

Sample answer:

To the editor:

I am writing in response to Principal Snyder's decision to turn certain required classes into distance education classes. I think this is a horrible idea. I understand that the principal is trying to save money to build a new gym, but it seems that he's willing to do so by sacrificing the quality of our education.

Since when is a videotape a good substitute for a teacher? With no teacher present to monitor students' progress, some students may get bored with the material quickly while others may have trouble keeping up. There will be no one there to gauge when it is appropriate to slow down or move on. What if we have questions about confusing material? If our teacher can only be seen on a monitor, there will be no one present to answer our questions and give us feedback on assignments and tests. There has to be a better way for the school district to save money than by reducing our teachers and classes to images from a distance.

Sincerely,

Terrell Warner

PART 1: *Reading*

Lesson 1: Recognition of a Theme or Central Idea

This lesson covers the following skills for reading and writing (Standard 3.1: G.21, B.11, and D.4):

- Identification, analysis, and application of knowledge of theme or central idea
- Use of supporting details and evidence from text and experience

For the reading section of this test, questions for these skills may be either multiple-choice or open-ended questions. You will do some prewriting before writing this essay. You will learn more about this portion of the test in **Part 2: Writing, Revising, and Viewing.**

What is the theme or central idea?

The **central** or **main idea** is the essential message of a passage. Sometimes the central idea is stated in a passage, meaning you can actually put your finger on a sentence or two expressing the central idea. Other times the central idea is not stated and you have to determine it from the information in the passage.

In narrative (fictional) passages, the central idea is called the **theme**. The theme is the overall message or impression the author is trying to convey. You won't be able to put your finger on a theme in a narrative passage. You have to read the passage to determine the theme.

Supporting details explain and expand the central idea or theme. They provide more information about the central idea or theme. Supporting details might be facts, examples, or descriptions.

Test questions about the central idea or theme might ask you what the passage is specifically about or what the passage is mainly about. They might also ask you to identify the main idea of a paragraph in the passage. Questions about supporting details may ask you which detail supports the author's main idea. They might also ask you to correctly identify supporting details in a passage. For example, you might be asked, "What causes the children to enter the house?"

 # Activity 1

Read the following paragraph. Think about the main idea, what the whole paragraph is about, as you read. Then fill in the graphic organizer underneath the paragraph.

Ancient Egyptian physicians were very advanced for their time, but some of their "cures" for illnesses and diseases were way off base. While these physicians had some clinical knowledge, meaning they based some of their treatment on science, they were also very superstitious and offered their patients magical cures. If you lived in ancient Egypt and had a stomach ache, your doctor might tell you to crush a hog's tooth and put it inside of a sugar cake and eat it. To cure a headache, your doctor would advise you to fry a catfish skull in oil and rub this oil on your head. If you had trouble with your eyes, your physician would mix together special ingredients, including parts of a pig, put the mixture in your ear, and say, "I have brought this thing and put it in its place. The crocodile is weak and powerless."

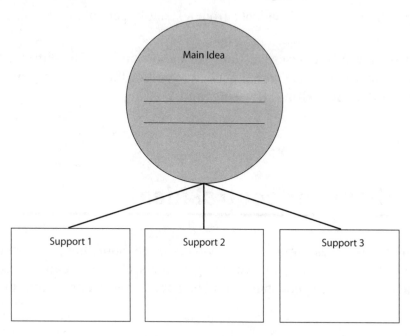

Activity 2

Break into groups of about four or five. Write a paragraph containing supporting details using one of the following sentences as the main idea.

- My summer vacation was really great last year.
- Sometimes you can learn an important lesson from making a big mistake.
- Heroes come in all shapes and sizes.

Passage 1

Now read this passage. Think about the main idea as you read. Then answer the questions that follow.

The Trail of Tears

One of the saddest events in the history of our nation was the forced removal of the Cherokee Indians from their homelands in the southeastern regions of the United States to the Oklahoma Territory in the Midwest. By the time the Cherokee reached Oklahoma, they had lost more than four thousand of their friends, relatives, and loved ones. The thousand-mile trail they left behind them came to be called "*Nunna dual Tsuny*," or "The Trail Where They Cried."

Principal Chief John Ross

In 1776, the United States declared its independence from Great Britain and set about establishing a new nation where all people were considered equal. The founding fathers of the United States drafted the Constitution in 1787 and by 1790 all thirteen of the original colonies had ratified the Constitution. Soon after, the new United States of America began to grow by leaps and bounds. Both population and territories increased. European settlers arrived in America and explored new lands. They pushed further into the frontier, forcing many Native American tribes from their homelands. By 1830, settlers had flooded into Georgia and increased the population of the state several times over. A large number of Cherokee Indians had lived in Georgia for many years before the settlers began to arrive, but their lives were about to change dramatically.

For a while, the settlers and the Cherokee shared the land and resided together peacefully. The Cherokee adapted to the European way of life that the settlers had brought with them to America. They adopted European dress, built roads, schools, and churches, and began raising cattle and farming. Some Cherokee Indians even married white settlers. The discovery of gold on Cherokee lands, however, prompted some settlers to urge the United States government to remove the Cherokee from their homeland. In 1830, the United States Congress passed the Indian Removal Act, which called for Native Americans to be removed from their lands in the east and transferred to lands in the west. The removal of Native American people from their home territories created more space for settlers and allowed them to take control of the valuable resources found on the land. While the removal was good for the settlers, it was devastating for the Native Americans. In 1832, the Cherokee won a small victory when the United States Supreme Court declared the removal laws invalid. The court said that the Cherokee belonged to their own nation and that the only way the United States could remove them from their lands was through a treaty.

By 1835, the Cherokee Nation was divided on removal practices. While the large majority of Cherokee Indians followed Principal Chief John Ross, a small number followed Major John Ridge. Ross wanted to negotiate with Congress. With the backing of the Cherokee council, Ross asked Congress to recognize the Cherokee people as full citizens of the United States with voting rights and representatives in Congress. In exchange for these rights, the Cherokee would agree to give up their land and voluntarily move west. Congress refused to grant the Cherokee these rights, however.

Major Ridge had a different plan for the Cherokee. On December 29, 1835, he assembled a small group of Cherokee leaders, none of whom belonged to the Cherokee council, and signed the Treaty of New Enchota. Even though most of the Cherokee people disagreed with the treaty and fought its passage through Congress, the treaty was passed in 1836 by one vote. It allowed President Andrew Jackson to order the removal of the Cherokee from their lands in the southeastern United States to the Oklahoma Territory.

General Winfield Scott

In May of 1838, General Winfield Scott and seven thousand men began rounding up the Cherokee from their homelands. Within a few weeks, they had captured or killed most of the Cherokee living in Georgia, Tennessee, and Alabama. The soldiers separated families and gave them little time to gather personal belongings and important possessions. Cherokee men, women, and children were gathered in shabby, disease-ridden camps with little shelter and food. Then, the Cherokee began the forced march, more than a thousand miles of rugged terrain and rushing rivers, from Georgia to Oklahoma during the fall and winter of 1838 and 1839.

The first groups of Cherokee to make the devastating journey lost many to disease and illness. John Ross asked General Scott to allow him to lead some of his people to the Oklahoma Territory and Scott agreed. Ross divided the people into smaller groups so they could travel separately and look for food along the way. While Ross managed to spare the lives of many of his people, it is estimated that approximately four thousand Cherokee died along the Trail of Tears. With little time to mourn the death of loved ones, the Cherokee labeled their march "*Nunna dual Tsuny*," or "The Trail Where They Cried." Today this trail is known as the Trail of Tears.

Lesson 1 **RECOGNITION OF THEME OR CENTRAL IDEA**

 Questions

1. Write a phrase telling what this passage is mostly about.

   _____

2. Now, write a sentence expressing the central idea of this passage.

   _____

   _____

3. Identify three supporting details in the passage.

   _____

   _____

   _____

   Check your answers on the next page. Read the explanation after each answer.

Passage 1: "The Trail of Tears"

 Answers

1. Your answer should contain a phrase, such as "Trail of Tears," or "Cherokee forced to move."

2. Your answer should contain a sentence stating what the passage is about, such as "The passage is mostly about the reasons the Cherokee were forced to move to Oklahoma and the pain they suffered during this move."

3. Remember that supporting details expand upon the main idea. Here are some supporting details, but there are others!

   a. The settlers urged the Unites States government to remove the Cherokee from their homeland when they discovered gold on the land.

   b. The removal was good for the settlers, but it was terrible for the Cherokee.

   c. When the Cherokee reached Oklahoma, they had lost more than four thousand of their loved ones.

Passage 2

Now read this passage. Think about the central idea as you read. Then answer the questions that follow.

The Ideal Bunkhouse

Alejandro kicked a stone across the sidewalk and sighed downheartedly. "I've had so much to do lately, between chores and schoolwork," he commented. "I'd love to go somewhere peaceful and just kick back and relax."

"Me, too," remarked Jerry. He reached into his pockets and pulled them inside-out. "I don't have enough money to take a vacation, though."

The two friends considered their predicament for a few moments, and then looked at each other and exclaimed in unison: "We'll build a new bunkhouse!"

Alejandro and Jerry had built a bunkhouse several years ago, but that one had been shoddy and unsophisticated—"very childish," was how Jerry described it. They had used old, knotted wood that they had excavated from a junk pile, and hammered it together clumsily. The roof leaked, one wall collapsed, and the door fell off completely; in short, their first bunkhouse was a disaster. Now that they were older and more knowledgeable, they knew they could do better.

The friends found a vacant yard behind their apartment building that seemed perfect for their new construction project. They consulted Mrs. Fernando, the owner of the land, and she gave them permission to build their bunkhouse there. Now they had a location and permission, and it seemed like no obstacles stood in their way. They raced to the yard, laughing excitedly.

"If we start now, we can finish in a few hours," Jerry concluded enthusiastically.

"No way," Alejandro protested. "Remember how we rushed to build the last bunkhouse and how badly it turned out?" Alejandro suggested dedicating more time to this latest endeavor to make it truly impressive. Jerry considered this idea and then agreed. "Now that that's resolved," said Alejandro, "let's split up and gather the materials we'll need." The two friends separated and rocketed off excitedly in different directions.

Alejandro headed directly to the local public library, where he searched the card catalog for titles on architecture. He gathered a pile of books. Flipping through their pages, he saw photographs and diagrams of some of the most magnificent buildings in the world. Some were museums, some were castles, some were skyscrapers, but they were all fine art to Alejandro's eyes. He wanted to build a massive, beautiful structure that would last for years—and to do that he would need to perform a lot more research.

He began brainstorming and wrote down a long list of topics he'd need to investigate, from plumbing to electricity to local laws. Then he went to work gathering information on each of these topics. Soon he had over a dozen books, and he intended to read every one of them before even starting to build the grandiose vacation resort he was imagining.

RECOGNITION OF THEME OR CENTRAL IDEA   Lesson 1

Meanwhile, Jerry had gone to the local hardware store, where he began searching for lumber, tools, and other supplies that he thought would be necessary for the project. He found some equipment that he thought would be perfect, but when he saw the prices, he started to feel uncertain. All the equipment he wanted was far too expensive. Jerry looked despairingly into his wallet and found barely enough money to purchase a single piece of lumber. "I'd need a million dollars to buy all the stuff I need here," he muttered. He was only very dejected for a moment, however, because he had a surefire alternative plan.

Jerry raced to his Uncle Jim's house. Just a week ago, Uncle Jim had arranged to have an old garage in his yard demolished. The remains of the garage—huge stacks of rotten wood and rusty nails—were stacked up and waiting to be discarded. Uncle Jim told Jerry he could take whatever he needed, and Jerry did exactly that. He gathered as much as he could carry and ran back to his and Alejandro's meeting place.

When the boys met again, they were surprised by the major disparity between the types of materials they had brought. Alejandro had furnished the project with fifteen library books and a notebook already half-filled with plans and theories. Jerry, on the other hand, had brought a pile of old knotted wood and bent nails. Immediately, the two began to quarrel. Alejandro accused Jerry of being sloppy, and Jerry accused Alejandro of being unrealistic.

"Don't you want to make the best bunkhouse we can?" Alejandro demanded.

"Don't you want to make something instead of reading all day?" Jerry countered.

After they'd argued for nearly an hour, they both started to appreciate the value in one another's ideas. Although Alejandro did have unrealistically high expectations, he was correct when he realized that the boys should do some research before they started to build the bunkhouse. And although Jerry was starting the project in a sloppy, haphazard way, he was correct that they shouldn't do so much planning that they failed to accomplish anything.

When they finished arguing, they devised a plan that satisfied them both. They would do some reading, but they would also put the wood to use. They worked together to construct two benches from the wood, and built a simple canopy to keep the hot sun out. Then they relaxed on the benches and read the library books. There they sat for many pleasant hours, planning the ideal bunkhouse that they would build another day.

Lesson 1 **RECOGNITION OF THEME OR CENTRAL IDEA**

Questions

1. What is this story mostly about?

   A. two boys who build wooden benches
   B. two boys who learn to work together
   C. two boys who live in the same apartment building
   D. two boys who built a bunkhouse several years ago

Tip
Some answer choices refer to supporting details in the story. While some of these details are true, they do not express the central idea. Choose the one that tells what the entire story is about.

2. "The Ideal Bunkhouse" is specifically about a struggle between

   A. planning and doing.
   B. new and old.
   C. neatness and sloppiness.
   D. boredom and excitement.

Tip
Think carefully about the theme of this story and how the two boys differ in their approach to building the bunkhouse. Why do they argue?

3. How does Alejandro's trip to the library contribute most to the central idea of the story?

   A. Alejandro learned that the boys could not build the bunkhouse without help.
   B. Alejandro became determined to build a quality, well-planned structure.
   C. Alejandro was late and there was little time to build anything.
   D. Alejandro met his grandfather at the library and they both researched carpentry.

Tip
This question asks you about a supporting detail in the passage. Go back and reread the passage. Where does Alejandro go?

4. What do the boys decide to do at the end of the story? Use details and information from the story to support your answer.

_____

_____

_____

_____

Tip
This question asks you about supporting details found at the end of the story. Re-read the end of the story. The boys argue, and then they come up with a plan using both of their ideas. What do they do?

Now check your answers on the next page. Read the explanations after each answer.

Passage 2: "The Ideal Bunkhouse"

 Answers

1. B   "The Ideal Bunkhouse" is about two boys working together. Alejandro and Jerry learn to overcome their differences and work toward building a new bunkhouse. Answer choice B is correct. While the other answer choices are true, they are supporting details in the story, and not the central idea.

2. A   The "Ideal Bunkhouse" is about a struggle between planning to do something and actually doing it. Alejandro wants to plan as much as possible before building the bunkhouse and Jerry wants to actually build it.

3. B   The central idea of the story is that the boys needed to join their individual visions for building the bunkhouse because each of them had different ideas on how to get started. Alejandro wanted to build a sturdy structure that wouldn't fall down and Jerry just wanted to get started. The response that best fits with this central idea is answer B.

4.   **Sample answer:** At the end of the story, the boys decide to put Jerry's wood to good use. They build benches and sit on them while reading the books Alejandro brought about building a bunkhouse. They agree to stop arguing and work together.

Passage 3

Now read this passage. Think about the central idea as you read. Then answer the questions that follow.

A Real Job

Damen Muñez carefully explained his current predicament to his mother: he was in the midst of a financial crisis—in other words, he had no money. He was off school for nearly two weeks for spring break and desperately wanted a temporary job to earn some money to put toward a new bike he had seen in a store window. "Even though I'm extremely responsible and bright," Damen explained and held his hands in front of him dramatically, "I'm only thirteen and no one on Earth will give me a chance."

Gabriella Muñez raised her eyebrows at her son and smiled. "What about me?" she asked. "You can work at the office this coming week. We have a huge deadline around the corner and could really use some extra help."

Damen could barely contain his excitement upon hearing his mother's words. "You want me . . . to work for you . . . at the office? I would ab-so-lute-ly love that—and you won't be sorry. I will work incredibly hard, I promise, and I will make you proud of me," Damen said.

His mother kissed him on the forehead. "I am already proud of you," she said, "but I think a real job would be a great experience. You can start on Monday."

Damen's mother was a book producer. She ran a small company that wrote and edited textbooks for publishers. Ever since they were little, Damen and his sister, Maria, had spent several hours each day at their mother's office, which had a kitchen in the back with a table where they completed their homework while enjoying a snack. Damen and Maria were fascinated with the many simultaneous projects their mother and her staff worked on and they loved being around creative individuals, hundreds of books, and modern computers and software. Damen had always wanted to work at his mother's company, but he never dreamed it would happen so soon. His mother had just given him a precious gift: a chance to use his outstanding writing skills to earn a paycheck. Damen contemplated his first assignment—he was a math whiz, so he figured he would probably be assigned to write a math textbook. He also loved to write science-fiction stories. Perhaps he would be writing a few of these, too.

When Damen and his mother arrived at the office Monday morning, the staff welcomed him aboard as their new "editorial assistant" and he felt truly honored. He had known most of the editors for many years, but he had never been allowed to work with them before.

Damen's mother explained that Matthew, an editor, needed some help fact-checking a social studies textbook. "I will check in with you before 1:00," she said, "when Grandma will pick you up."

"What?!" Damen scoffed. "Why can't I work the whole day, like you and the other editors?"

Gabriella chuckled. "You will be tired by 1:00, señor just you wait and see," she said.

Lesson 1 **RECOGNITION OF THEME OR CENTRAL IDEA**

Matthew politely guided Damen to a table in his office and spread out the materials he would need for his first assignment: a printout of the textbook from the designer, a pen, and a computer with a CD in it. Matthew explained that Damen was to verify each highlighted fact in the textbook on the CD and if it wasn't available on the CD, Damen was to check it online. *This is a piece of cake*, Damen thought—until he saw the number of highlighted facts on each page. "I'm supposed to check every one of these?" he asked Matthew, who just smiled and nodded.

Damen quickly realized that verifying each fact was no easy task. He could verify some information easily on the CD, but other facts, like the dates for major events in Mesopotamia, had to be verified online using only credible university websites, which made his task even more daunting.

After about an hour, Damen asked Matthew if he could take a break and stretch and Matthew agreed that this was a good idea. Damen headed downstairs to the kitchen, where his mother was stirring milk in her coffee. Damen told his mother about his work and asked if there was any way possible he could switch to an assignment requiring writing, but she just grinned. "You have to learn to walk before you can run, Damen," she explained, "and besides, work is just that—work—and you have to learn to do what needs to be done without complaint."

Damen reluctantly returned to his workstation and continued his task. Every so often he would look and up and see the other editors typing quickly, answering phone calls, and walking from office to office with folders and books. He wondered how they managed to complete tedious tasks, like the one he was doing, while still managing to be creative when necessary. He also wondered how they could keep track of so many things at once without losing their sanity. They made their jobs look easy, but Damen was realizing that being an editor was actually very difficult.

When the clock struck one, Damen had a headache, his eyes were blurry, his back ached, he had ink all over his hands, and his stomach was growling. Frustrated, he told Matthew that he had only managed to verify the facts in the first few chapters of the book. "That's good!" exclaimed Matthew. "You're a great help. You can pick up where you left off tomorrow."

When Damen descended the stairs, his mother was waiting for him. "Mom," he said, "I don't think I did so well. I had to fact-check a social studies book and I don't think I got as much done as I should have."

"Did you do a good job?" asked his mother.

Damen explained that he knew the facts he had checked were correct, but that it was very tedious and difficult work.

Mrs. Muñez raised her eyebrows. "Ah," she said. "You're not quitting, are you?"

"No!" Damen replied. "I'm just trying to figure out how I can do a better job tomorrow."

Mrs. Muñez smiled and told Damen that she was very proud of him. "If I didn't know you and you were hired as an editorial assistant here and had such a positive attitude, I'd be thrilled," she said.

RECOGNITION OF THEME OR CENTRAL IDEA **Lesson 1**

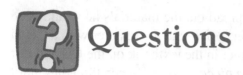 Questions

1. What did Damen learn from working at his mother's office?

   A. Being an editorial assistant is hard work.
   B. His mother's office is not as fun as he once thought.
   C. Fact-checking is not as fun as writing.
   D. Saving up money for a bike takes a long time.

 Tip

This question asks you about the central theme of the story. What is the main thing that Damen learns from working as an editorial assistant at his mother's office?

2. What causes Damen to think he did a bad job?

   A. His mother tells him he is leaving at 1:00.
   B. His mother will not give him a chance to write.
   C. He had to verify many facts online.
   D. He has taken a long time to do his work.

 Tip

This question asks about a supporting detail in the passage. Why does Damen tell his mother he believes he has done a bad job?

Lesson 1 **RECOGNITION OF THEME OR CENTRAL IDEA**

3. What does Damen imagine his first assignment will be?

    A. writing a math book
    B. writing a social studies book
    C. fact-checking a social studies book
    D. assisting Matthew with his work

 Tip
This question asks about a supporting detail. Go back and reread the part of the story where Damen thinks about his first assignment.

4. What does Damen plan to do on his next day of work?

    A. try harder to do a better job
    B. use a CD to help him with his work
    C. ask his mother for a new assignment
    D. talk to Matthew about his problem

 Tip
Reread the end of the story to find this supporting detail.

Check your answers on the next page. Read the explanation after each answer.

RECOGNITION OF THEME OR CENTRAL IDEA **Lesson 1**

Passage 3: "A Real Job"

 Answers

1. A The major lesson that Damen learns is that being an editorial assistant or an editor is difficult work. At first he thinks his job will be fun, but he then learns that it can be tedious and difficult.

2. D At the end of the story, Damen tells his mother that he didn't get as much work done as he probably should have. This is the reason he thinks he did a bad job.

3. A When Damen imagines his first assignment at his mother's office, he thinks he may be writing a math book or a science-fiction story. Answer choice A is the correct answer.

4. A At the end of the story, Damen tells his mother he is trying to figure out how he can do a better job tomorrow. Answer choice A is the correct answer.

Passage 4

Now read this informational passage. Then answer the questions that follow.

A *Pop*-ular Kind of Corn

Every weekend, millions of Americans pile into cinemas to see the latest movies. As they enter the theater, they are greeted by the familiar aroma of buttered popcorn. Their noses lure them to the concession stand to buy a bag of the buttery snack. What these anxious moviegoers may not realize as they devour the salty, butter-drenched treat is that popcorn has been a popular snack for centuries.

Archaeologists, scientists who study fossils and artifacts to learn about ancient cultures, have actually studied ancient popcorn. Scientists discovered ancient kernels of popcorn in many parts of the world. The oldest ears of popcorn ever discovered were found in New Mexico's Bat Cave in 1948 and 1950. The ears were believed to be somewhere between three thousand and six thousand years old! Other discoveries have also led scientists to confirm popcorn's old age. Eighty-thousand-year-old fossil corn pollens were found buried beneath what is now Mexico City in Mexico, and ancient popcorn pots made of clay were found in Peru, a country in South America. Christopher Columbus recorded that natives in the West Indies gave popcorn to his sailors when he landed there in 1492. Popcorn was an important source of food for the Aztec Indians of Mexico. They also used popcorn in special ceremonies to honor their gods. Native Americans were planting, harvesting, and eating popcorn long before the Pilgrims arrived in America. But early colonists found a new way to enjoy popcorn—as a breakfast cereal. They served popcorn with sugar and cream.

From the early 1900s to the present, popcorn has been a staple of fairs, carnivals, circuses, and theaters. Even during the Great Depression, when many families were very poor, popcorn remained an affordable treat. During World War II a sugar shortage slowed candy production, but Americans responded by increasing the amount of popcorn they ate. Today, popcorn is still a favorite among many people.

Even though popcorn was an important part of many ancient cultures from different parts of the world, today much of it is grown in the United States. States such as Illinois, Ohio, and Nebraska are known for producing some of the world's best popcorn. Nebraska is even nicknamed the "Cornhusker State." It usually takes about ten days for popcorn plants to emerge from the ground after the seeds are planted. The plant eventually grows to about eight feet tall, and produces ears of corn covered with green husks. Once the plants turn brown and dry, the popcorn is harvested.

RECOGNITION OF THEME OR CENTRAL IDEA Lesson 1

Each kernel of popcorn has the potential to become one of those mouth-watering morsels we munch on during a movie. Popcorn kernels are made up of three main parts: the endosperm, the germ, and the pericarp. The endosperm is whitish in color, is made mostly of starch, and surrounds the germ. The germ is found near the pointy end of a popcorn kernel. The pericarp, also called the hull, is the hard, outer shell. A small amount of moisture is found within the endosperm. When popcorn kernels are heated, the moisture becomes a vapor, much like when you boil water on a stove. But unlike water on the stove, the vapor inside the popcorn kernel is not released into the air, and pressure within the kernel builds as the temperature rises. When the kernel reaches about five hundred degrees, the kernel explodes to release the vapor and turns itself inside out. The white, starchy substance from the center of the kernel is now on the outside, and the hard outer shell becomes the center.

Throughout its history, popcorn has seen many changes in the way it is prepared. Some ancient cultures dropped popcorn kernels into sand heated over a fire. Others had clay pots with legs that stood over the fire allowing the popcorn to be heated. Winnebago Indians cooked popcorn by placing an ear of popcorn on a stick and holding it near a fire, allowing the corn to pop right on the cob! The first mechanical popcorn machine was invented in 1885, and today people use air poppers, microwaves, or stoves to cook popcorn.

Lesson 1 **RECOGNITION OF THEME OR CENTRAL IDEA**

 Questions

1.   This passage is mainly about

   A.   the history of popcorn.
   B.   ancient uses for popcorn.
   C.   how popcorn has changed.
   D.   different uses for popcorn.

 Tip
Look for the answer that applies to the entire passage.

2.   Which sentence gives the best summary of the article?

   A.   Popcorn is often sold at fairs, carnivals, circuses, and theaters.
   B.   Popcorn has been enjoyed by many different cultures for thousands of years.
   C.   While ancient cultures grew corn, most popcorn today is made from corn grown in the United States.
   D.   Native Americans planted, harvested, and ate popcorn even before the Pilgrims arrived in America.

 Tip
To answer this question correctly, look for the choice that covers the most important point in the passage.

3.   From the passage, describe TWO ways popcorn was cooked in the past.

_____

 Tip
Go back and reread the article before answering this question.

Check your answers on the next page.

RECOGNITION OF THEME OR CENTRAL IDEA   **Lesson 1**

Passage 4: A *Pop*-ular Kind of Corn

 Answers

1. A Three of the answer choices for this question are supporting details, but the entire passage—the central idea of the passage—is about the history of popcorn.

2. B A summary of a passage includes the most important point or points. Three of the choices provide supporting ideas that develop the central idea of the passage. The best summary is answer choice B.

3. **Sample answer:** Some ancient cultures cooked popcorn kernels by dropping them into sand and cooking them over a fire. Others heated popcorn in clay pots, which they placed over a fire. The Winnebago Indians cooked popcorn by letting it pop right on the cob.

Lesson 2: Paraphrasing/Retelling and Making Tentative Predictions of Meaning

This lesson covers the following skills for reading (3.1: E.1, G.9, and G.11):

- Paraphrasing/retelling
- Making tentative predictions of meaning

For the reading section of this test, questions for these skills may be either multiple-choice or open-ended questions. This essay is longer than an open-ended question. You will do some prewriting before writing this essay. You will learn more about this portion of the test in **Part 2: Writing, Revising, and Viewing**.

What is paraphrasing/retelling?

For questions asking you to paraphrase/retell a word or a phrase from a passage, you have to choose the answer choice that is closest in meaning. You should look at the **context**, the way the word or phrase is used in the passage, to help you figure out its meaning. Often the sentence the word is used in will be given to you in the question. Other times, the number of the paragraph the word is used in will be given. For example, a question might ask, "In paragraph 2, <u>division</u> means—"

What is making tentative predictions of meaning?

Questions asking you to predict the meaning will most often cite a phrase or sentence from a passage and ask you to choose the answer choice that best expresses the author's meaning. For example, a question might ask, "In paragraph 2, what does the author mean when she says 'Obviously, a division between parties was inevitable.'" You have to read the passage carefully to answer these types of questions. Sometimes, their meaning isn't literal. The author might be being humorous or sarcastic.

Activity

Try to figure out the meaning of these words from the way they are used in each sentence. Look the words up in a dictionary to check your answers.

- With seven siblings and twenty-six cousins, Matt had a *plethora* of relatives.

- All that remained of the small boat was some *flotsam* floating on top of the water.

- Shaking her head, Shelley admitted the location of her missing notebook was an unsolvable *conundrum*.

- Under the *tutelage* of my older sister Michelle, I finally learned to swim.

- Nan, Lil, Bob, and Ava are names that are examples of *palindromes*.

Passage 1

Now read this passage. Then answer the questions that follow.

Daffodils
by William Wordsworth

I wander'd lonely as a cloud
That floats on high o'er vales and hills,
When all at once I saw a crowd,
A host, of golden daffodils;
Beside the lake, beneath the trees,
Fluttering and dancing in the breeze.

<u>Continuous</u> as the stars that shine
And twinkle on the Milky Way,
They stretch'd in never-ending line
Along the margin of a bay:
Ten thousand saw I at a glance,
Tossing their heads in sprightly dance.

Lesson 2 **PARAPHRASING AND PREDICTING MEANING**

The waves beside them danced; but they
Out-did the sparkling waves in glee:
A poet could not but be gay,
In such a jocund company:
I gazed—and gazed—but little thought
What wealth the show to me had brought:

For oft, when on my couch I lie
In vacant or in <u>pensive</u> mood,
They flash upon that inward eye
Which is the bliss of solitude;
And then my heart with pleasure fills,
And dances with the daffodils.

 Questions

1. Read these lines from the poem.

    Ten thousand saw I at a glance,
    Tossing their heads in sprightly dance.

    What does the author mean by this?

    _____

    _____

2. What does the word "continuous" mean in this poem?

    _____

    _____

3. What do you think the word "pensive" means in this poem?

    _____

    _____

PARAPHRASING AND PREDICTING MEANING Lesson 2

Passage 1: "Daffodils"

 Answers

1. **Sample answer:** The author means that he saw thousands of daffodils blowing in the breeze, which made them look as if they were dancing.

2. **Sample answer:** "Continuous" means endless and ongoing. The poet is comparing the daffodils to the endless amount of stars in the sky.

3. **Sample answer:** "Pensive" means thoughtful. The sentence in which this word is used gives a clue. The author says that when he lies on the couch and feels pensive, his mind wanders to memories of the flowers.

Passage 2

Now read this passage about the history of golf. Then answer the questions that follow.

The Birth of Golf

Hundreds of years ago, most people relied on the land in order to survive. They would spend many hours every day growing crops, gathering wood, and herding animals. Since they spent their days largely out-of-doors, they were of course surrounded by rocks and sticks. It seems only natural that, when they found a few minutes for recreation, they would create games using this makeshift equipment.

Many historians believe that as far back as the reign of Julius Caesar around 2,000 years ago, people were playing a game that involved striking a round pebble or a ball with a tree branch. However, it wasn't until the Middle Ages that this sort of game became very popular. Around 1400, many countries throughout Europe had adopted variations of this simple pastime. The Dutch and Irish played it on the ice of their frozen lakes and canals. This game, called Shinty or Hurling, resembled modern-day hockey.

Other people of other nationalities played differently, but the most unique version of the game developed in eastern Scotland in the 1400s. Here, as legend has it, bored shepherds took up the club-and-ball pastime as many others before them had. However, the geographic characteristics of the Scottish coast—which included grassy tracks, sand dunes, and, most importantly, rabbit holes—made these shepherds' game very special. The shepherds not only hit the pebbles, but they practiced aiming and swinging in order to send the pebbles far out into the meadows—and into the rabbit holes. Whoever could get the pebble into the rabbit hole with the least amount of swings was the winner. The Scottish shepherds called this pastime "gowf."

Once the idea of adding holes spread throughout Europe, most people modified the games they'd been playing. The game became more popular than ever. Soon, England had "goff," the Netherlands had "kolf," and France and Belgium had their own variations. Royalty and peasants alike wanted to participate in this new sport, which would evolve over generations into what we know today as golf.

5 The game made an impact immediately. It was immensely popular with the citizens of Scotland, who were so enthusiastic about the game that they devoted much of their time to it. They spent so much time playing sports like golf that they neglected their duty to King James II; specifically, they shrugged off their obligation to train for the military. The enraged king, seeing his military might suffering because of the people's obsession with sticks and pebbles, declared golf illegal in 1457!

PARAPHRASING AND PREDICTING MEANING | Lesson 2

Even a royal reproach was not enough to stop the Scottish people from enjoying their sport. They created golf courses, called links, along the sandy seashores of their nation. People flocked to these links day in and day out. The most popular course was named St. Andrews. At its beginning it was just a single small tract of land surrounded by bushes and heather shrubs; as more and more people visited it, it began to grow tremendously. The visiting golfers brought business to the surrounding cities, and suddenly there was a great call for golf clubs, balls, as well as caddies (golfers' assistants). The owners of St. Andrews worked over the next generations to expand their golf course, and today it is the largest golfing complex in Europe. At the time, however, golf was still illegal!

7 The outlook for the new sport brightened almost 50 years later, when King James IV decided the banned pastime was actually quite entertaining. Not only did he lift the ban, but his interest in the sport—like a celebrity endorsement today—made golf more popular than ever. King James himself began playing golf in 1502; in fact, some believe that he was the first person to officially purchase a full set of golf clubs. The royalty of England and Scotland began teaching foreign rulers how to golf.

The sport took a strong hold in France; however, the heart of golf remained in Scotland. The capitol of the country, Edinburgh, hosted the world's most famous golf course, called Leith. In 1744, the first golfers' organization, the Gentleman Golfers, formed at Leith. They originated the idea of golf tournaments, yearly competitions featuring impressive trophy prizes. Additionally, they devised a set of rules for the game that was widely accepted.

Golf had come a long way since the sticks and stones used in the 1400s. In 1618, a special golf ball was created, made of feathers instead of stone; it was called, understandably, the "Featherie." Featheries were so difficult to make that each one was often more expensive than a club! It was a relief to many golfers when less expensive balls were later mass-produced out of cheaper materials, like rubber. By the 1700s, specially designed clubs and balls were being handcrafted by exclusive shops. The club handles were made mostly from special kinds of wood. Many early clubs also had heads made of wood, though some heads were made of blacksmith-forged iron. Today, most clubs are made entirely of lightweight, super-strong metal.

 Questions

1. In the first paragraph, the author says people played games using <u>makeshift equipment</u>. This means that the equipment was

   A. durable.
   B. special.
   C. professional.
   D. homemade.

Lesson 2 **PARAPHRASING AND PREDICTING MEANING**

Tip

Remember that people first played golf with sticks and stones. What kind of equipment is this?

2. In paragraph 5, what does the author mean when he says people "shrugged off their obligation to train for the military"?

   A. They were not sure if they were supposed to train for the military.
   B. They did not bother to train for the military even though they were supposed to.
   C. They played games while they participated in the military.
   D. They were sent away to participate in the military.

Tip

Go back and reread the paragraph. What were the people doing? What were they supposed to have been doing?

3. In paragraph 7, the author writes, "The outlook for the new sport <u>brightened</u> again almost fifty years later, when King James IV discovered that the banned pastime was actually quite entertaining."

   What is the meaning of <u>brightened</u> in this sentence?

   A. lit up
   B. improved
   C. opened
   D. cheered up

Check your answers on the next page. Read the explanation after each answer choice.

Passage 2: "The Birth of Golf"

 Answers

1. D   The "equipment" was really sticks and stones that the people made into equipment. Therefore, the best answer choice is D.

2. B   The author means that people were so busy playing golf that they did not train for the military even though they were supposed to. Answer choice B is the best answer.

3. B   While all of the answer choices could be definitions of the word "brightened," in this passage "brightened" means "improved."

Passage 3

Now read this passage about reality television. Then answer the questions that follow.

The "Reality" of Reality Television

1 The American people have suffered long enough: it's time to put an end to reality television. In recent years, reality television shows have become a staple of many networks' programming schedules and it's easy to see why. Reality television offers a glimpse into the lives of people just like you and me. Rather than watching a scripted television show where a famous actor or actress portrays a normal, ordinary person, we can watch normal, ordinary people receive the star treatment, compete in outrageous contests, and win exorbitant amounts of money. Who wouldn't want to live in a "reality" where you can increase your bank account by a few thousand dollars simply by swimming with a few snakes or parachuting out of a plane?

Reality television does have some advantages over traditional scripted television shows. There seems to be an endless supply of topics from which to choose, and an endless amount of people willing to step up and take on the newest challenge. There's always some new show waiting in the wings, ready to humiliate a new cast of characters and spark the interest of a new group of viewers. From the corporate world to hospital operating tables to boxing rings, it seems that reality television cameras are everywhere, witnessing everything. As long as the cameras catch a few laughs, a few cries, and a few fights, producers can take months of footage and piece together several hours of fast-paced, exciting television. Reality shows take less time, effort, and money to create than  scripted television shows. There's usually one big pay-off at the end of the show where the winner gets an amazing prize, instead of five or six actors and actresses who are paid high salaries per episode. Despite these few positive aspects, most reality television shows are littered with problems.

Perhaps the main problem with reality television is best demonstrated through a comparison of actual reality and television reality. In the early days of film, filmmakers created documentaries about real people and events in history. For example, a filmmaker might show how Inuit people living in Alaska hunt for caribou. Another filmmaker might capture the ancient rituals of an African tribe or show the effects of poverty in a Third World country. When these documentaries were shown on television, viewers could see how ordinary people living in the real world are affected by real circumstances. These documentaries served as educational tools by showing the actual reality that some people must face. The difference between this reality and today's reality television shows is that today's shows have lost the concept of "reality." Reality shows that set out to represent real life situations that could affect anyone at any time have morphed into outrageous contests that focus on the extremes people will go to get what they want. Can it be considered "reality" to drop a bunch of strangers on an island with no food or water and force them to compete for a million dollars? Is it reality to participate in all kinds of crazy

tests in order to be crowned the head of a successful corporation? Television reality shows are less about real life and more about the best way to surprise a member of the cast and shock viewers at home.

Today's reality shows no longer offer us a real glimpse into the lives of people and cultures from around the world. We don't get to see how people really live, work, and interact with others. We don't get to hear their innermost thoughts and feelings, or see their ways of life. Instead, most of today's reality television shows offer viewers a cast of characters who live in a tent, on an island, or in some magnificent mansion. These people participate in funny, foolish, or outlandish acts to win money, cars, jobs, modeling contracts, recording contracts, and even future spouses. **4** They will do whatever it takes to have their fifteen minutes of fame. These shows pit friend against friend, husband against wife, and family against family, all in the name of entertainment. But what happens when these shows are over and these people try to return to their normal lives? Is it possible for them to go back to their old lives when their words and actions have been immortalized on the television screen for the whole world to see?

It is a shame that this form of television, which could be used to educate the world about so many important issues, is more often used as an expanded dating game or the road to superstardom. Instead of teaching us about the reality of what it's like to grow up as a minority, reality shows teach us how to put a puzzle together with our toes while wearing a blindfold. Reality shows could focus on important issues that people deal with in real life: finding a job after high school or college; volunteering for a community organization; or learning how to perform a new skill. Instead, most "reality shows" give us a group of people taking time out from their normal, everyday lives to take part in some fantastic scheme created by a television producer. And the last time I checked, that wasn't reality.

 Questions

1. In paragraph 1, <u>staple</u> means

    A. fasten.
    B. clip.
    C. necessity.
    D. pin.

 Tip

Go back to paragraph 1 and reread the sentence containing the word "staple." What does it mean?

Lesson 2   PARAPHRASING AND PREDICTING MEANING

2. What does <u>interact</u> mean in paragraph 4?

   A. communicate
   B. care about
   C. understand
   D. know about

Tip
Go back and reread paragraph 4. The sentence containing the word should give you a clue.

3. What does the author mean in the last paragraph when she says, "...reality shows teach us how to put a puzzle together with our toes while wearing a blindfold"?

   A. Reality shows teach us many new and interesting things.
   B. Reality shows teach us about outrageous things.
   C. Reality shows are sometimes hard to understand.
   D. Reality shows are only appreciated by some people.

Tip
Reread the last paragraph. What message is the author trying to convey?

Check your answers on the next page. Read the explanation after each answer choice.

Passage 3: "The 'Reality' of Reality Television"

 # Answers

1. C   In this passage, staple means "necessity." Some television networks consider reality shows to be a necessary part of their programming.

2. A   The sentence that the word "interact" appears in says that "We don't get to see how people really, live, work, and interact . . ." Answer choice A, "communicate," is the best answer choice.

3. B   The best answer choice is B: Reality shows teach us about outrageous things. The author stresses that reality shows do not teach us about anything useful.

Passage 4

Now read this passage and answer the questions that follow.

Excerpt from *The Old Curiosity Shop*
by Charles Dickens

One night I had roamed into the City, and was walking slowly on in my usual way, musing upon a great many things, when I . . . turned hastily round and found at my elbow a pretty little girl, who begged to be directed to a certain street at a considerable distance, and indeed in quite another quarter of the town.

"It is a very long way from here," said I, "my child."

"I know that, sir," she replied timidly. "I am afraid it is a very long way, for I came from there to-night."

"Alone?" said I, in some surprise.

"Oh, yes, I don't mind that, but I am a little frightened now, for I had lost my road."

"And what made you ask it of me? Suppose I should tell you wrong?"

"I am sure you will not do that," said the little creature, "you are such a very old gentleman, and walk so slow yourself."

I cannot describe how much I was impressed by this appeal and the energy with which it was made, which brought a tear into the child's clear eye, and made her slight figure tremble as she looked up into my face.

"Come," said I, "I'll take you there."

She put her hand in mind as confidingly as if she had known me from her cradle, and we trudged away together. . . .

"Who has sent you so far by yourself?" said I.

"Someone who is very kind to me, sir."

"And what have you been doing?"

"That, I must not tell," said the child firmly.

There was something in the manner of this reply which caused me to look at the little creature with an involuntary expression of surprise; for I wondered what kind of errand it might be that occasioned her to be prepared for questioning. Her quick eye seemed to read my thoughts, for as it met mine she added that there was no harm in what she had been doing, but it was a great secret—a secret which she did not

PARAPHRASING AND PREDICTING MEANING   Lesson 2

even know herself. . . . She walked on as before, growing more familiar with me as we proceeded and talking cheerfully by the way, but she said no more about her home. . . . It was not until we arrived in the street itself that she knew where we were. Clapping her hands with pleasure and running on before me for a short distance, my little acquaintance stopped at a door and remained on the step till I came up knocked at it when I joined her. . . . There was a noise as if some person were moving inside, and at length a faint light appeared through the glass [and] an old man with long grey hair, whose face and figure as he held the light above his head and looked before him as he approached, I could plainly see. . . . The place through which he made his way at leisure was one of those receptacles for old and curious things which seem to crouch in odd corners of this town and to hide their musty treasures from the public eye in jealousy and distrust. There were suits of mail standing like ghosts in armour here and there, fantastic carvings . . . rusty weapons of various kinds, distorted figures in china and wood and iron and ivory: tapestry and strange furniture that might have been designed in dreams. . . .

[T]he child addressed him as grandfather, and told him the little story of our companionship.

"Why, bless thee, child," said the old man, patting her on the head, "how couldst thou miss thy way? What if I had lost thee, Nell!"

"I would have found my way back to YOU, grandfather," said the child boldly; "never fear."

The old man kissed her, then turning to me and begging me to walk in, I did so. The door was closed and locked. Preceding me with the light, he led me through the place I had already seen from without, into a small sitting-room behind, in which was another door opening into a kind of closet, where I saw a little bed that a fairy might have slept in, it looked so very small and was so prettily arranged. The child took a candle and tripped into this little room, leaving the old man and me together.

"You must be tired, sir," said he as he placed a chair near the fire, "how can I thank you?"

"By taking more care of your grandchild another time, my good friend," I replied.

"More care!" said the old man in a shrill voice, "more care of Nelly! Why, who ever loved a child as I love Nell?"

He said this with such evident surprise that I was perplexed what answer to make. . . . I was surprised to see the child standing patiently by with a cloak upon her arm, and in her hand a hat, and stick.

"Those are not mine, my dear," said I.

"No," returned the child, "they are grandfather's."

[She] cheerfully helped the old man with his cloak, and when he was ready took a candle to light us out. . . . [The old man] walked on at a slow pace. . . . I remained standing on the spot where he had left me, unwilling to depart. . . . [I] could not tear myself away, thinking of all possible harm that might happen to the child. . . .

Lesson 2 **PARAPHRASING AND PREDICTING MEANING**

[A]ll that night, waking or in my sleep, the same thoughts recurred and the same images retained possession of my brain. I had ever before me the old dark murky rooms—the gaunt suits of mail with their ghostly silent air—the faces all awry, grinning from wood and stone—the dust and rust and worm that lives in wood—and alone in the midst of all this lumber and decay and ugly age, the beautiful child in her gentle slumber, smiling through her light and sunny dreams.

 Questions

1. Read this sentence from the passage:

   There was something in the manner of this reply which caused me to look at the little creature with an involuntary expression of surprise; for I wondered what kind of errand it might be that occasioned her to be prepared for questioning.

   In this sentence, the word <u>involuntary</u> means

   A. frightened.
   B. unintentional.
   C. disgusted.
   D. bored.

 Tip
Picture the look of surprise on the narrator's face as he wondered what the little girl had been doing on the streets at night all alone. How might surprise affect a person's facial expression? How does he feel about this little girl? If you aren't sure, go back and read this part of the story.

2. At the end of the story, the narrator pictures the girl "alone in the midst of all this lumber and decay and ugly age." The word <u>midst</u> means

   A. confusion.
   B. dust.
   C. middle.
   D. pile.

Tip

Try to see in your mind what the narrator is seeing in his. Where is the little girl? Substitute each of the answer choices for the word "midst" to see which one makes the most sense.

3. Shortly after meeting the little girl, the narrator tells the reader that he "wondered what kind of errand it might be that occasioned her to be prepared for questioning." As it is used here, the word <u>occasioned</u> means

    A.   parted.
    B.   caused
    C.   suffered.
    D.   wanted.

Tip

Find this sentence in the passage and read this section of the story. What is the narrator wondering about the little girl? Which answer choice makes the most sense?

Check your answers with those on the next page. Read the explanation after each answer.

Passage 4: Excerpt from "The Old Curiosity Shop"

 Answers

1. B   The story does not suggest that the narrator is frightened by the little girl, nor does it say anything that would lead the reader to believe he was disgusted. He is certainly not bored by the little girl's secrecy. Consider how similar the word "involuntary" is to the word "volunteer." A volunteer chooses to do something. A *voluntary* action is intentional, or chosen. Therefore, an action that is *involuntary* is an unintentional action. The narrator does not mean to look surprised, but people who are surprised often reveal emotions that they did not mean to show.

2. C   The narrator pictures the little girl sleeping in the middle of all the strange objects and "musty treasures" he saw when the old man let him into the shop. Answer choice C makes the most sense.

3. B   The narrator wonders what the little girl has been doing and what caused her to reply that her activities were a secret. This is the only answer choice that makes sense in the context of the story.

Lesson 3: Recognition of Text Organization and Purpose for Reading, Extrapolation of Information/Following Directions

This lesson covers the following skills for reading (3.1: A.1, E.6, G.18, G.20, and G.21):

- Recognition of text organization
- Recognition of a purpose for reading
- Extrapolation of information/following directions

For the reading section of this test, questions for these skills may be either multiple-choice or open-ended questions. This essay is longer than an open-ended question. You will do some prewriting before writing this essay. You will learn more about this portion of the test in **Part 2: Writing, Revising, and Viewing**.

What is recognition of text organization and purpose?

Authors create pieces of writing for many reasons. They might write a short story to entertain readers or to teach a lesson. They might write an article that gives readers information or teaches them how to do something. Authors sometimes write persuasive articles or letters to convince readers to feel as they do or to persuade them to take a certain action.

Questions asking you to recognize text organization and author's purpose will ask you why authors structured their writing the way that they did. For example, you might be asked why an author included an anecdote (story) in the introduction of a persuasive piece. You might have to decide if a passage is meant to inform, instruct, entertain, or persuade.

How do you extrapolate information?

Some questions on the ASK8 will ask you to extrapolate information from a passage. When you **extrapolate** information, you expand upon what you have read in the passage either to clarify meaning or to incorporate your own personal experiences. For example, this type of question might ask you why a character in a short story acted a certain way. To answer a question like this, you might have to infer or predict why a character acted a certain way based on information in the story.

Activity 1

Determine the author's purpose for each sentence or group of sentences below. Write **entertain, inform, teach,** or **persuade** in the left-hand column.

Author's Purpose	Sentence
1.	It rained three inches yesterday.
2.	Everyone should recycle unwanted paper.
3.	Once upon a time, there lived a happy little rabbit named Bounce.
4.	Before you begin cleaning your room, you should get rid of all unnecessary clutter.
5.	The author George Eliot was actually a woman writing under a pen name.

Activity 2

In groups of 4 or 5 students, write a convincing advertisement for "Pearly White Toothpaste." Be sure to use persuasive words.

Passage 1

Read the following passage and answer the questions that follow.

Cutting Class Size

"Falling through the cracks" sounds like a scary prospect—and it is. For thousands of students in America, overcrowding in their schools is making their educational experience more straining and less effective. Promising students are falling through the cracks each day. They get lost in the crowd and never receive the individual attention and stimulation they need to reach their full potential.

Fortunately, there is a solution to this predicament. Reducing class size in America's schools is the best method by which we can eliminate these "cracks" in the educational system. This will be a challenging process, but many leading educators have developed a detailed plan to make it a reality.

Where It Should Start

The process should begin in the country's more troubled schools, in which the students' achievements have been consistently lower than average. These schools require special attention, and, by instituting small class size policies, they will receive it. The initial step would be to deliver adequate funding to these troubled schools, which will allow them to hire more well-qualified teachers and provide additional classroom space for the students. Once there is enough room to breathe, and enough concerned, properly trained teachers, the possibilities for the students are endless!

Classes of fifteen to twenty students would be ideal; that ratio of students per teacher would allow more individual attention for each student. Providing this reduced class size would greatly reduce many of the public's concerns about the United States educational system.

Putting Names on Faces

Students and parents alike have been worried by the sense of namelessness that exists in many modern schools. Under the current system, some students are just faces in a crowded classroom. If they aren't exceptional in an obvious way—such as being especially outgoing, academic, or athletic—they will likely be overlooked by their teachers and made to feel like nobodies. For instance, quiet students, no matter how talented they may be, are automatically at a big disadvantage. This is simply because they're harder to notice in a crowded room.

The namelessness problem is usually not a teacher's fault. Many teachers have to work with over a hundred different students per day, as well as manage troublemakers, do paperwork, and, of course, try their best to teach! It can be difficult to remember a hundred names, never mind any more personal details. And it can be impossible to notice small changes in individual students that might indicate more serious problems.

A reduction in class size could resolve these problems quickly. Teachers would have a much easier time getting to know their students, not just recognizing their faces. If a teacher knows a student's strengths and weaknesses, personality and interests, it will vastly improve that student's academic and personal experience. The teacher will be better able to help him or her, as well as communicate in more effective, meaningful ways.

Less Muss, Less Fuss

For many students, the experience of attending overcrowded classes can be a miserable one. With thirty or more students confined in a small room, problems are inescapable. Even if everyone is cooperating, there will be some noise, confusion, and delays. If a student doesn't understand the material and would benefit from another explanation, he or she might be hesitant to ask the teacher for a recap because the remainder of the class might want to move on.

If everyone isn't cooperating, there can be chaos, like yelling, fighting, cheating—all types of problems. It can make the classroom a stressful, depressing place to be. Students who are willing to follow the lesson are distracted and annoyed by other students. Students who don't want to follow the lesson can't be convinced to do so, because the teachers lack the time or resources to properly deal with them.

Smaller classes would eliminate these problems. With fewer students, there will almost certainly be reduced noise and distraction. A teacher will be able to guide the class much more easily, not having to shout over voices and spend valuable time trying to discipline troublemakers.

Our Best Bet

Of course, there are people opposed to the idea of reducing class sizes in America's schools. These critics mostly point to the problems of funding these significant changes. They are correct in that it would be a costly endeavor, but would it be worth the investment? Some critics have presented the challenge that small class size would not guarantee that the students will improve their performance in school. That may be true, but only because it depends on the students and their cooperation!

However, few could claim that the ideals of the small class size plan are deficient. A policy that allows students more access to instructors, and lets instructors become more familiar with students, promises to have a great positive effect on our nation's schools.

TEXT ORGANIZATION AND PURPOSE
Lesson 3

? Questions

1. Why do you think the author wrote this passage?

   _____

   _____

2. According to the article, how will reducing class size help students?

   _____

   _____

3. Read these sentences from the introduction of the passage.

   "Falling through the cracks" sounds like a scary prospect—and it is. For thousands of students in America, overcrowding in their schools is making their educational experience more straining and less effective.

   Based on these sentences, what does the author want to show about children in overcrowded schools?

   _____

   _____

   _____

   Check your answers on the next page.

Passage 1: "Cutting Class Size"

 Answers

1.   **Sample answer:** The author wrote "Cutting Class Size" to persuade readers that reducing class size is good for students.

2.   **Sample answer:** The author believes that reducing class size will help students in several ways. It would help teachers get to know students better, so students are not just nameless faces in a crowd. It would also reduce distractions as well as help teachers and students communicate more effectively.

3.   **Sample answer:** The author is trying to show that students who do not receive the attention they need at school are seriously harmed and that many students in American schools today do not receive this attention.

Passage 2

Read this narrative passage. Then answer the questions that follow.

A Costly Lesson

In just three short months, Gabriella would begin high school. She was excited about this important transition and saw it not only as a chance to change schools, but also as a graduation from childhood. Walking around her room, she surveyed her possessions and contemplated her life. Suddenly, she felt disappointed by her slow progression into adulthood. "Look at all these kiddy things," she commented, glowering at the stuffed animals and picture books she had had since she was a toddler. "I need to get rid of all of this and redesign myself."

Over the weekend Gabriella found some boxes and began stacking all her old toys and books in them. It was exciting to see her shelves becoming clear and to imagine all the grownup things she would accumulate in the upcoming years to fill them.

She was so excited, in fact, that she did not pay close attention to what she was doing. Only for one instant did she hesitate, and that was when she paused to look at a worn purple bear she had treasured as a baby. It had little circular paws, whiskers, and an optimistic smile. She had named it Oscar and lugged it with her wherever she roamed. Now Oscar was a bit battered and threadbare from all her affection, which she noticed just before she dropped it into the box. *Maybe the second-hand store could sell old Oscar for fifty cents*, she thought. Since the money would be contributed to charity, it seemed like a great deal all around.

When Gabriella had packed all of her childhood possessions into the boxes, she taped the lids shut and carried them to the drop-off window at the second-hand store. She placed the heavy parcels down with a thud. A worker there thanked her for her donation and then carried the boxes into a storage room. Gabriella strode away feeling refreshed and very mature.

Although her room was almost empty now, she thought it had great potential for becoming a young woman's room and would suit her well now that she was nearly grown up. The shelves were empty except for the dust that had fallen between her outdated, former possessions. She retrieved some towels and mopped up the dust and then sat on her bed as she imagined some of the remarkable new things she could gather and display on the shelf. No ideas came to her immediately, but she figured they would soon enough. Satisfied, she lay back on the bed and fell asleep.

Gabriella awoke during the middle of the night and was unable to fall asleep again. Tonight the moonlight was too bright on her face; normally it was blocked by the stuffed animals on the shelf above her head. Gabriella sat up and examined the shelf, which appeared empty and lifeless. *Oh well*, she thought with a shrug, *at least it's more adult now*. Then she collapsed back down onto the pillows, though she remained too restless to sleep well.

In the morning she was not only exhausted but downhearted and felt as though something was missing. The sensation was so uncomfortable that she just couldn't ignore it. Throughout the afternoon, she wondered if her decision to get rid of her old things had been a good one. Her room definitely looked more mature now, but it also looked barren. Gabriella decided that, just out of curiosity, she would stroll downtown to the second-hand store and see if they had transferred her donations to the sales floor yet.

Upon arrival, she found Oscar already offered for sale. But instead of being heaped into the toy bin with the regular stuffed animals, Oscar was encased in a glass display unit in the front of the store. Staring closely, she was astounded to see that the price of the bear was $40! Confused, she questioned one of the employees, who explained that he had recognized the bear as being from a special series of toys that went out of production years ago. Not many bears like Oscar had been manufactured and those that had were now prized collectors' items. While Oscar was a little battered, he was still valuable property.

The employee continued, "In fact, a collectibles dealer will be arriving later today to buy him. He'll probably end up residing in a display window at a big-city specialty store."

Shocked and dismayed, Gabriella suddenly realized what she had to do. She pulled out the money she had saved to buy grownup things from her wallet and she bought back her old companion, Oscar. When she arrived home, her mother inquired as to her whereabouts.

Gabriella explained, "I learned an important lesson today. Adults don't have to discard everything from their pasts." Then she proudly returned Oscar to his rightful position on her shelf.

Questions

1. Which adjective would the author use to describe Oscar?

    A. shared
    B. precious
    C. ordinary
    D. general

Tip
This question asks you to extrapolate information from the passage to choose the adjective that bests describes Oscar. Think about how Gabriella feels about Oscar and what she does to get him back.

TEXT ORGANIZATION AND PURPOSE   **Lesson 3**

2. Why did the author write this story?

   A. to convince readers not to give away items from their childhood
   B. to entertain readers with a story about a girl who learns a lesson
   C. to explain why a tattered bear was worth a lot of money
   D. to teach readers a lesson about growing up too quickly

 Tip

Think about what the author's purpose was in writing this story. Then eliminate incorrect answer choices.

3. Why does Gabriella want to change her room?

_____

_____

_____

_____

Now check your answers with those on the next page. Read the explanation after each answer.

Passage 2: "A Costly Lesson"

 Answers

1. B Oscar is important to Gabriella, so much so that she uses her savings to buy him back from the second-hand store. The best answer choice is B, "precious."

2. B Since this is a story, its purpose is to entertain. The author does not try to persuade readers, and the article is not informational. While the story does teach a lesson, Gabriella learns the lesson. The author was not really trying to teach readers a lesson.

3. **Sample answer:** Gabriella wanted to change her room because she was about to begin high school and was no longer a young child. She thinks high school marks the end of her childhood and feels that her room should look more grown-up. This motivates her to get rid of her childhood treasures.

Passage 3

Read the following passage. Then answer the questions that follow.

Space Colonization: Too Big a Risk

Imagine spending your entire life in a space suit hooked up to a machine that gives you the air you need to breathe. Imagine living in temperatures colder than any place on Earth—even Antarctica. Sound like fun? Obviously not. Yet supporters of space colonization are working hard to ensure that people inhabit outer space during our lifetime. This is no longer just a wild science fiction tale. Advances in technology and recent scientific discoveries about places beyond our planet may have actually paved the way for the establishment of the first space colony.

Many people are enthusiastic about this idea, and see it as an entirely positive opportunity for the people of Earth. While supporters of space colonization believe that colonizing another planet would be one of the biggest steps ever taken in human history, they are overlooking the dangers and expenses of such an endeavor.

First of all, the complications of establishing a livable city on another planet are staggering. Even the world's finest scientists are still baffled by the question of how they could keep people safe and healthy on the surface of an alien world. People require very special conditions in order to live, and it would be hard to ensure those conditions on an unexplored new world.

Of all the planets, Mars seems like it would best support human visitors—but it's still an inhospitable place. The atmosphere is so thin it would be impossible to breathe. People would need special equipment in order to get the air they need to live. It's possible that the first colonists would have to spend their entire lives wearing space suits. Also, temperatures on the red planet can become extremely cold, far colder than even the most frigid places on Earth. It might be possible for people to live in such temperatures, but few would find them comfortable.

Although there may have once been flowing water on Mars, today it is a very dry planet. Humans rely on water to live, and colonists would have to bring a large amount of it with them. Special machines would have to be developed in order to recycle the drinking water. Even if the water problem was solved, how would the colonists get food? The Martian ground is rocky and dry; it seems unlikely that any kind of Earth crops could possibly grow there. Until people discovered a way to grow crops, rockets would have to be constantly sent to the colony with fresh supplies. The cost of doing this would be huge.

Additionally, the overall cost of a colonization mission would be downright breathtaking. Scientists have estimated the price tag of a single mission to be about $30 billion. This funding is desperately needed for projects here on our own planet. Social programs of all sorts could benefit greatly from even a fraction of that amount. We humans would be wise to invest more time, money, and effort in improving our own world before we start visiting others.

We must also consider a sad, but important, question: can humans be trusted with a brand new planet? Humans have proven to be very imperfect guests, to say the least. The greatest threats to our current planet are posed by us, its inhabitants. Through weapons, warfare, pollution, and greed, humanity has taken advantage of the natural splendor that Earth once possessed. Some scientists believe that humans have a duty to spread out across the solar system and spread beauty and intelligence. However, over the centuries humans have spread just as much hatred and horror as they've spread beauty and intelligence.

Some supporters of space colonization believe that the nations of Earth would unify and work together to achieve this common goal. These supporters think that all aspects of Earth life, from education to economics, would be improved by the race to colonize space. However, a short survey of history points to the contrary.

History shows that colonization has caused greed, hatred, prejudice, and war among the nations of Earth. Imagine the effects of space colonization! Nations would likely struggle to be first to reach the red planet; then they would struggle for the rights to build on the best land; then they would struggle for resources for their colonists. This could result in further mistrust, fear, and conflict. A Mars colony might end up further dividing the people of Earth and yielding more suffering than discovery.

Should a colonization project proceed despite these many problems, what sort of benefits would it bring to the people of Earth? Some scientists have suggested that we build mines in space to gather valuable metals like iron and gold from asteroids and other celestial bodies. This would return some of the costs of the mission. However, our planet is already well equipped with dozens of types of metal and minerals. In fact, with Earth's natural resources as well as our recycling programs, we have more than enough already. Besides, if we were to build colonies just to make money, greedy competition would no doubt arise that would endanger the whole project.

Some scientists have proclaimed that colonizing the red planet would ensure the survival of the human race. Their argument is that, even if Earth were to die or be destroyed, a group of humans would still exist in their Martian colony. This argument may be true, but it's not convincing because it doesn't apply to our world's current situation. Earth is still a healthy and vital planet and promises to remain that way for a very long time. The human race is growing every year and is definitely not endangered. Generations of humans can live for millions of years longer on Earth—if only we learn to behave more responsibly.

In conclusion, the concept of space colonization is a fascinating one, but it is fraught with problems and dangers. There may be a time when humans are ready to build their cities on the surface of Mars. However, attempting to conquer Mars now, while neglecting Earth, might bring enormous damage to Earth and its inhabitants.

TEXT ORGANIZATION AND PURPOSE Lesson 3

Questions

1. In paragraph 1, why does the author describe what it would be like to live in space?

    A. to prove that humans will one day be able to live in space
    B. to show that some people strongly support humans living in space
    C. to convince readers that living in space would be uncomfortable
    D. to show that humans still have a lot to learn about life in space

Tip
This question asks you about the organization of the passage. Think about what kind of passage this is and the image the author creates in the first paragraph.

2. Though "Space Colonization: Too Big a Risk" is about one person's thoughts on space colonization, it would be useful background reading for an oral report on

    A. the weather in Antarctica.
    B. what it is like on Mars.
    C. problems on Earth.
    D. how cities are built.

Tip
Which answer choice is discussed most throughout the article?

3. Which word would the author use to describe people who support space colonization?

   A. uninformed
   B. irresponsible
   C. unskilled
   D. considerate

Tip

The author feels strongly that humans should not establish a space colony. What does he say about those who support this?

4. Why does the author think it's a bad idea to spend so much money on space colonization?

   A. Not enough is known about space colonization.
   B. We should spend money where it is most needed.
   C. Too many people are afraid to live on other planets.
   D. It might cause resentment among people in other nations.

Tip

Reread the part of the article where the author discusses the amount of money it would cost for a single mission. Why does he think it's a bad idea to spend so much money on space colonization?

Check your answers on the next page. Read the explanation after each answer.

Passage 3: "Space Colonization: Too Big a Risk"

 Answers

1. C   The author describes what it would be like living in space in paragraph 1 to show how uncomfortable it would be and to convince readers not to support the establishment of a space colony.

2. B   In addition to space colonization, the author gives information about the planet Mars, such as facts about its temperature, soil, and air.

3. B   The author thinks that space colonization is a bad idea because it is unsafe and costs too much money. Therefore, the best answer choice is B, "irresponsible."

4. B   The author thinks the money spent on space colonization should be used to help people on earth. Answer choice B is the best answer choice.

Passage 4

Read this informational passage. Then answer the questions that follow.

New Jersey: A Land of Liberty

New Jersey is nicknamed "the Garden State," but it would be more fitting to call it "the Liberty State," since New Jersey has long served as a gateway to freedom. If you look across the river from New Jersey's Liberty State Park, well-known land-marks dot the horizon and the Statue of Liberty and the New York City skyline loom in the distance. Ellis Island, a large part of which lies in New Jersey, is home to the immigration station where many immigrants first registered in America. These sites, so closely tied to New Jersey, once held dreams of freedom and independence for the many immigrants traveling to America. Throughout history, New Jersey has been closely associated with symbols of freedom such as the Declaration of Independence, the Statue of Liberty, and Ellis Island.

Finding Freedom

On July 4, 1776, the founding fathers of the United States signed the Declaration of Independence, which freed America from British control. American colonists set about to establish a new, democratic republic where "all men are created equal" and where everyone has the right to "Life, Liberty and the Pursuit of Happiness." In 1787, New Jersey became the third state to approve the new Constitution, behind only Delaware and Pennsylvania.

As America grew, it became a symbol of freedom and independence to people in other countries. In honor of the United States' one hundredth birthday in 1876, the French dedicated a gift as a token of their friendship and respect. This gift, which still stands in New York Harbor about two thousand feet from Liberty State Park, was the Statue of Liberty. French scholar Edouard de Laboulaye came up with the idea for the massive copper statue and sculptor Auguste Bartholdi created the masterpiece. Lady Liberty holds a tablet engraved with the date of America's independence in her left hand. In her right, she holds the torch that lights the way to liberty. Broken shackles by her feet represent freedom from tyranny. This incredible symbol of freedom was often the first sight that immigrants saw as they entered New York Harbor on crowded ships.

Immigration for Independence

Between 1892 and 1924, immigration in the United States was at its peak. The main immigration station in the United States was located on Ellis Island. The original Ellis Island registration building was destroyed by fire in 1897, but a new one was constructed in its place and opened in 1900. Ferryboats carried immigrants from stuffy, cramped steamships to the immigration station. Some immigrants came for new jobs and opportunities, while others fled their home countries because of religious or political persecution. At the immigration station, immigrants waited for hours in long

lines that stretched from the docks in the harbor, into the main building, and up several flights of stairs to the Registry Room. As the immigrants made their way through the line they were given a medical examination to determine if they had any serious diseases or disabilities. When they finally reached the Registry Room, they told immigration workers their names, where they were from, where they were going, and how much money they had. Between 1900 and 1914, about five thousand to seven thousand immigrants were processed at Ellis Island each day, and millions more entered America at Ellis Island before the immigration station closed its doors in 1954.

Locomotive to Liberty

As immigrants left Ellis Island, some headed for New York, but others bought tickets to board the Central Railroad of New Jersey (CRRNJ) and traveled on the train to their new homes. As the population of the United States increased throughout the 1800s, the need for railway transportation in New Jersey became more obvious. The area where Liberty State Park now stands was once one of the busiest industrial areas of New Jersey. Small railroads hauled freight and passengers in and out of New Jersey. Then, in 1849, two railroads—the Elizabethtown and Somerville Railroad and the Somerville and Easton Railroad—combined to form the CRRNJ. In 1864, the CRRNJ built its first railroad terminal where people could purchase tickets and board trains. In 1866, the CRRNJ leased a portion of the Lehigh and Susquehanna Railroad, which stretched from Easton, New Jersey to Wilkes-Barre, Pennsylvania. Soon, the railroad began hauling anthracite coal in addition to its normal freight and passengers. As immigration increased, a second terminal was constructed in 1889. This terminal, located near what is now the northern part of Liberty State Park, still stands today as an important part of American history. Between 1890 and 1915, approximately forty thousand people and three hundred trains arrived at and departed from the CRRNJ terminal every day.

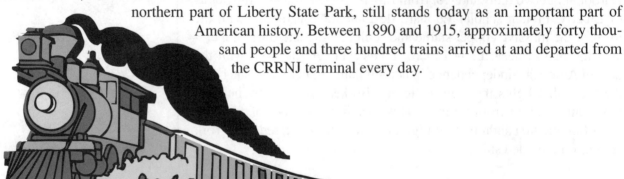

The CRRNJ remained in operation until the 1930s. The track stretched for more than seven hundred miles at the peak of the railroad's success. The immigration laws and the Great Depression took their toll on the CRRNJ, however. Eventually it was taken over by a large corporation, but parts of the original track were closed. Today, a visit to Liberty State Park wouldn't be complete without a tour of the CRRNJ terminal to see where many immigrants hopped aboard a locomotive to liberty.

Liberty State Park

New Jersey's Liberty State Park officially opened on June 14, 1976, in honor of the nation's two hundredth birthday. The park lies at the edge of the Hudson River on the eastern border of New Jersey and spans more than 1,200 acres, most of which is open space. From the shore, visitors can take in the breathtaking view of Ellis Island, the Statue of Liberty, and the New York City skyline. The CRRNJ terminal, once bustling with hopeful immigrants, is situated at the northern end of the park. It is here where many immigrants first set foot on the mainland of the United States ready to board a train or meet family members and begin the next step toward establishing a life in America. Today, ferryboats carry visitors from the park to the Statue of Liberty and Ellis Island.

 Questions

1. According to the article, people are often not aware that New Jersey

    A. played an important role in the establishment of America.
    B. was the first state to sign the Declaration of Independence.
    C. had a population made up largely of immigrants coming to America.
    D. assisted with the construction of the Statue of Liberty.

 Tip

Reread the beginning of the article. Why does the author think that New Jersey should be called the "Liberty State"?

2. Why did the author write this article?

   A. to inform readers of New Jersey's connection to freedom
   B. to persuade readers that New Jersey is a great place to live
   C. to entertain readers with a story about the history of New Jersey
   D. to show readers why New Jersey was important to immigrants

Tip

Eliminate answer choices that are obviously incorrect. Then think about the central idea of this article. What information was the author trying to convey to readers?

3. Why was the Central Railroad of New Jersey (CRRNJ) built?

   A. to take people to visit the Statue of Liberty and Ellis Island
   B. to transport many people in and out of New Jersey
   C. to help immigrants travel safely to America
   D. to haul anthracite coal from New Jersey to Pennsylvania

Tip

Reread the information in the article under the subheading "Locomotive to Liberty."

4. Under what heading did you find the information to answer #3?

   A. Finding Freedom
   B. Immigration for Independence
   C. Locomotive to Liberty
   D. Liberty State Park

Check your answers on the next page. Read the explanation after each answer.

Passage 4: "New Jersey: A Land of Liberty"

 Answers

1. A   In the beginning of the article, the author says that New Jersey should be called the "Liberty State" even though most people call it the "Garden State." The article goes on to explain New Jersey's contributions to the development of America.

2. A   The author wrote the article to inform readers that New Jersey is closely connected to freedom and liberty—the main reasons so many immigrants came to America.

3. B   The article says that when many immigrants came to America, New Jersey needed a way to get people in and out of the state. While answer choice D is a true statement, coal was not hauled on the railroad when it was first built, so this was not the reason the railroad was built.

4. C   This question is based on the location of information from the passage. The previous question contains the topic you need to locate—The Central Railroad of New Jersey (CRRNJ). Information on this topic is found under the heading, "Locomotive to Liberty," answer choice C.

Lesson 4: Making Judgments, Forming Opinions, and Drawing Conclusions

This lesson covers the following skills for reading (3.1: E.1 and G.11):

- Making judgments
- Forming opinions
- Drawing conclusions

For the reading section of this test, questions for these skills may be either multiple-choice or open-ended questions. This essay is longer than an open-ended question. You will do some prewriting before writing this essay. You will learn more about this portion of the test in **Part 2: Writing, Revising, and Viewing**.

How do you make judgments, form opinions, and draw conclusions?

Questions on the ASK8 that ask you to make judgments, form opinions, and draw conclusions have one thing in common: You will not be able to look back at a passage and put your finger on the answer. For these questions, you have to use the information and details you have read in the story to come up with the correct answer.

Some questions on the ASK8 will ask you to **make a judgment** about what you have read. These types of questions may ask you to put yourself in the place of a character and predict what you would do in a similar situation.

Questions asking you to **form an opinion** will ask you to reach beyond what you have read and form an opinion about it. For example, you might be asked to identify additional information that would fit in with the story, as in this question: "Ken's older brother and younger sister are able to accept the family's move to Boston, but Ken is distressed with the idea. Give TWO more reasons why a middle-school student might not want to move. Describe how Ken is able to resolve this problem."

Drawing conclusions questions will ask you to decide something based on what you have read. For example, you might be asked why a character performs a certain action or why an author feels the way he or she does about a subject.

Activity

Not everything in print is a reliable source. In groups of four or five, imagine you are writing a biography of a famous person. Select a person, and list some sources that would provide accurate information. Then, list some sources in which the information might not be accurate. Share your group's findings with the class.

Passage 1

Read this advertisement. Then answer the questions that follow.

Center City Science Adventure

Have you ever wondered about the journey of a red blood cell as it gathers oxygen from the lungs and distributes it to other parts of your body? Have you ever thought about how thunderstorms form or how the nitrogen cycle works? If so, the Center City Science Adventure is the perfect place for you to experience science up close and personal.

Since 1997, Center City Science Adventure has established a reputation as an entertaining, educational expedition through the world of science. We pride ourselves on our massive, state-of-the-art replicas of human organ systems, our guided tours to the "center of the Earth," and our magnificent Milky Way Galaxy model. Join us today and experience the wonder and amazement of our bodies, our minds, and our universe!

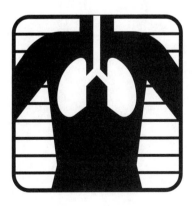

Center City Science Adventure
727 Wright Street
Center City
(555) SCI-ENCE

Take Exit 21A off Interstate 74W.
Turn left at the stop sign and follow
Wright St. to Main Ave.

CHECK OUT OUR EXHILARATING EXHIBITS!

THE HUMAN BODY Tours:	SOLAR SYSTEM Tours:	EARTH SCIENCE Tours:
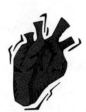		
Circulation Respiration Digestion Muscles and Bones Ears and Eyes	The Eight Planets The Moon The Sun Comets and Asteroids Stars	Under the Sea Earth's Cycles Greenhouse Effect Weather Phenomena Center of the Earth

Reserve your place on one of our daily excursions through the wonderful world of science. Parties of eight or more, please call to register at least two weeks in advance. **See our special rates for school field trips below.**

CENTER CITY SCIENCE ADVENTURE PRICE GUIDE

3-tour package	$15.00/person
6-tour package	$25.00/person
9-tour package	$35.00/person
2-day pass (all tours)	$50.00/person
Field trip special (5 tours)	**$9.00/child; $12.00/teacher or chaperone**

Questions

1. What kind of person would enjoy visiting the Center City Science Center?

   _____

   _____

   _____

2. Would you enjoy visiting the Center City Science Center? Why or why not?

   _____

   _____

   _____

3. Which exhibit do you think is probably the most popular? Why?

   _____

   _____

   _____

   Check your answers on the next page.

Passage 1: "Center City Science Adventure"

 **Answers**

1. **Sample answer:** A person who enjoys science and wants to learn about the earth, the human body, and outer space would enjoy visiting the Center City Science Adventure.

2. **Sample answer:** I would definitely enjoy visiting the Center City Science Adventure. The exhibits seem fun and fascinating.

3. **Sample answer:** I think the space exhibit is probably the most popular because people are fascinated with life on other planets. Most of my friends enjoy learning about the stars and other planets, and I think this exhibit would be the most interesting.

Passage 2

Now read this informational passage. Then answer the questions that follow.

The Truth about Organ Donation

Myths about organ donation have circulated for decades, but most are simply stories invented by people who don't understand the process of organ donation. The truth is that the organs donated from one person's body can save multiple lives. The heart, kidneys, pancreas, lungs, and intestines all can be donated. In addition, eyes and body tissues, such as skin and bone marrow, can be donated. In the United States alone, more than 87,000 people are on a waiting list to receive an organ, and these people may wait days, weeks, months, or even years, to receive an organ transplant. It is estimated that about ten to fourteen thousand people who die each year meet the requirements to be organ donors, but only about half of those people actually become organ donors. It is essential that you understand the facts about organ donation, so you can make the right choice when the time comes.

It might not be pleasant to think about what happens to a person's body after he or she passes away, but organ donors know that their organs will be used to save human lives. Many organ donors are victims of accidents or other unexpected traumas, and their organs are perfectly healthy when they arrive in the emergency room. Emergency room doctors work hard to save patients' lives, but sometimes the brain has been so severely damaged that it will never work again. If the brain shows no signs of activity and has no blood supply, doctors consider the brain dead, and the patient becomes a candidate for organ donation.

When a patient's family consents to donate the organs to someone in need, the patient is called a "donor." Doctors enter the organ donor's height, weight, and blood type into a computer, which searches for potential matches. The Organ Procurement and Transplantation Network maintains a list of people in need of organs. When a match is found, the patient who will receive the organ is prepared for the transplant surgery. A special team of physicians removes the necessary organs from the organ donor's body. Organs don't last very long outside the body, so once they have been removed they are quickly transported to the hospital where another surgical team is prepared to operate on the organ recipient. In some cases, the patient is ready to leave the hospital just a few days after the transplant surgery, but other times it takes longer for the patient to recover. Either way, most patients can eventually return to their normal lives, and live for many long, healthy years—all because a stranger was selfless enough to donate his or her organs to help save a life.

Becoming an organ donor is relatively easy; anyone, from a newborn baby to a great-great-grand-mother, can become an organ donor. In many states, you can declare your organ donor status when you receive or renew your driver's license. You can also complete and carry an organ donor card in your wallet. If you choose to become an organ donor, you should talk to your family about your decision, and make them aware that if something happens to you, you want to donate your organs. Remember, when you make the decision to become an organ donor, you make the decision to save a life.

 Questions

1. Which of the following is a reason why only half of the people eligible to donate organs actually donate them?

    A. People do not like to think about their own death.
    B. Organs donated from one person can save multiple lives.
    C. Once removed, organs do not last long outside the body.
    D. The process of becoming a donor takes a long time.

 Tip

If you're not sure of the answer, reread the article. Which choice reflects a conclusion someone could make about organ donations?

2. Why is it a good idea to inform your family if you decide to become an organ donor?

    A. to give them an opportunity to talk you out of it
    B. to be sure they know you want to donate your organs
    C. to convince them they should become organ donors too
    D. to help them understand the myths about organ donation

 Tip

Find and re-read the paragraph that explains how to become an organ donor.

3. Do you think more people will donate organs in the future?

 Tip

Think of the people you know and how they might react once they learn the fact about organ donation.

Check your answers on the next page. Read the explanation after each answer.

Lesson 4 **FORM OPINIONS AND DRAW CONCLUSIONS**

Passage 2: "The Truth about Organ Donation"

 Answers

1. **A** Choices B and C gives facts about organ donation. Choice C contradicts the first sentence in the final paragraph. Answer choice A is the only answer that gives a reason why someone would not be an organ donor.

2. **B** The passage promotes the importance of organ donation, so choice A does not fit. Choices C and D make important points about organ donation, but not reasons why you should talk to your family once you decide to become an organ donor. Therefore, answer choice B is the best answer.

3. **Sample answer:** I think more people will become organ donors in the future. As more people receive organ transplants and live longer than ever before, more people will learn about organ donations either through the news or because they know of someone who received a transplant. Soon more people will begin to realize that donating their organs is important and can save another person's life.

Passage 3

Now read this informational passage. Then answer the questions that follow.

Arachnid Addresses

Spider webs are a familiar sight because they appear to be everywhere—in houses, in yards, on signposts, on porches, and in some unexpected places as well. Most people consider them a nuisance, but did you ever stop to attentively examine a spider web? Each spider web is unique, and some are amazingly intricate. Next time you see a spider web, don't just glance at it—take a closer look!

Why Does a Spider Make a Web?

A spider's web is its residence, but it also serves as a snare or trap for beetles, flies, crickets, and other insects, as well as small animals such as birds and bats, which appeal to some large, powerful spiders. Spiders have teeth but they cannot chew, which means that they do not actually devour their prey, but drink the insect's or animal's fluids instead. Not all spiders require a web to capture their prey, such as the ground-hunting wolf spider, which pursues and pounces on its prey, but many spiders do make webs. This is sometimes the only evidence that spiders are present at all.

Different spider species make different webs.

Orb Webs

The most familiar type of web is called the *orb web*. It is made by spiders such as the golden orb web spider and the garden orb web spider and is recognizable by its wheel shape. Several strands called radii (singular: *radius*) stem from the hub, or center, of the web, and then several strands are laid over each radius in a circular pattern. This process is performed at night and can take several hours, depending on the size of the web. Some orb webs can span nineteen feet in height and six and a half feet in width!

Constructed to catch flying insects, most of the orb web is made from sticky spider silk. When an insect is caught in the adhesive strands, it becomes entangled and struggles to get free, creating vibrations that alert the spider—that often resides in the hub—that it has caught prey. Some spiders, such as the golden orb web spider, can spin a web strong enough to catch a small bird, which often demolishes the web in an effort to break free. Most spiders are too small to eat a meal so substantial, so to prevent damage to their webs, spiders frequently leave a trail of dead insects along the web so that birds and other animals will notice the web and evade it. Other spiders, however, devour large meals and will endeavor to bind the bird with silk threads so that it cannot flee. If a web is damaged in the struggle, the orb weaver spider often deconstructs the old web, regains its energy on a nearby bush or tree during the day, and then rises at nighttime to build a fresh web.

Lesson 4 **FORM OPINIONS AND DRAW CONCLUSIONS**

Funnel Webs

The funnel web is a horizontal web, meaning it lays flat instead of extending from top to bottom. Spiders such as the Sydney funnel-web spider, found mainly in Australia, usually make funnel webs in moist, sheltered places, such as under a rock or fallen tree. Underneath the flat sheet of web is a sequence of funnels, or tunnels, that lead to a hole where the spider is concealed. When an insect strolls out onto the web's smooth surface, the spider senses the vibrations, instantly emerges from the hole, bites the insect, and drags its meal back into the hole through the tunnels. Sometimes funnel-web spiders hunt on the surface of the web at night, but most often they stay in the funnel because this is the best place to remain hidden from prey. Funnel webs are very durable, and spiders that construct them often build on them for years. If you see a giant funnel web, you can be certain that the spider inside has been around for a while.

Sheet Webs

Sheet webs are made of a perplexing maze of threads that do not appear to follow a pattern, but they are very large and effective. From above, sheet webs resemble funnel webs, but they do not have a sequence of tunnels beneath. They extend between blades of grass, plants, or trees, depending on the size of the spider. The sheet web spider also constructs a net of threads above the web, so that flying insects are stopped by the barrier and will fall, stunned, onto the sheet. The spider, which waits below the sheet, then pulls the insect down through the sheet, and when the spider is finished feasting, it repairs the damage to the sheet, which is why sheet webs can last for a long time. Some spiders, such as the poisonous black house spider, create sheets that are several layers thick.

Cobwebs

The cobweb has an even more irregular design than the sheet web. Cobwebs can often be seen in ceiling corners, but they can also be constructed on bushes and the sides of houses and barns. Like the sheet web weavers, cobweb weavers sometimes build a net above their webs to catch flying insects while the spider waits nearby or behind the web. The spider then sprints out, binds its victim, and feasts. Many house spiders make cobwebs, but the famous and deadly black widow spider is also a cobweb weaver. Not all spiders are dangerous, but if you see a black widow, stay away!

FORM OPINIONS AND DRAW CONCLUSIONS | Lesson 4

 Questions

1. How does the author feel about spiders?

   A. terrified
   B. indifferent
   C. fascinated
   D. angry

 Tip
Think about the tone of this article. Then eliminate incorrect answer choices.

2. What type of spider would you most likely find in an attic?

   A. orb web spider
   B. funnel-web spider
   C. ground-hunting wolf spider
   D. house spider

 Tip
Go back and read about each of these spiders before drawing your conclusion.

3. The article says that different species of spiders make different types of webs.

   ● Describe ONE similarity and ONE difference between orb webs and sheet webs.

   ● Describe TWO ways that webs can capture prey.

Use details and information from the article to support your answer.

Check your answers on the next page. Read the explanation after each answer.

Lesson 4 **FORM OPINIONS AND DRAW CONCLUSIONS**

Passage 3: "Arachnid Addresses"

 Answers

1.   C   The author seems to be very intrigued by spiders. The author does not indicate fear, anger, or indifference toward spiders. Therefore, answer choice C is the best answer choice.

2.   D   The article says that house spiders make cobwebs, which are often seen in ceiling corners. Therefore, this is the best answer choice.

3.   **Sample answer:** Both orb webs and sheet webs are designed to catch flying insects. However, while orb webs are delicate and easily damaged, sheet webs are durable and can be repaired.

        Some spiders create webs made from sticky silk. When prey fly into such webs, they become tangled in the silk strands and cannot get free. Other spiders create strong sheetlike webs. When prey walk or fall onto these webs, the spider can sense the vibration, and it reaches up and pulls its prey through the sheet.

Passage 4

Now read this informational passage. Then answer the questions that follow.

The Emerald Isle

Known for its rolling green landscape, rainy climate, and rich history, an island about the size of West Virginia sits in the Atlantic Ocean and is often referred to as the "Emerald Isle." Its borders also touch the Celtic Sea and the Irish Sea, and its capital is Dublin. This island is the country called Ireland.

The island of Ireland is separated into two parts. The southern part of the country is called the Republic of Ireland, and the northern part is suitably referred to as Northern Ireland. Northern Ireland is part of the United Kingdom, a group of countries on another nearby island, including England, Scotland, and Wales, as well as a few smaller islands. While Northern Ireland is governed under British laws, the Republic of Ireland is independent.

Much of Ireland's coast is lined with low mountains, while the middle of the island is a combination of flat plains and rolling wetlands. Because water-laden coastal winds cause the weather to be very rainy all year, the country is famous for its wetlands, called bogs, where many different plants grow in rich shades of green, including many different types of clovers. According to ancient Irish history, finding a four-leaf clover hidden among the regular three-leafed variety is said to be lucky. The Irish countryside, which includes farmlands as well as bogs, is often enclosed in a dense white fog.

The earliest Irish were primarily farmers, who struggled to produce enough food to feed their families and pay farmland rent to their British landlords. Around the year 1600, the potato crop was introduced to Irish farmers, who instantly loved the potato because it thrived in many different conditions and could

feed many, many people. The potato became the most widespread food in Ireland, and its abundance enabled the population to grow. Then, in 1845, a deadly fungus spread through most of Ireland's potato crops, causing them to rot and turn black. The Irish people lost their main source of food, and the famine continued for years, causing many people to die of starvation. Some tried to eat different types of plants and grasses, while others left the country and made new lives in Canada and America, causing Ireland's population to drop drastically.

Today, Ireland has developed a healthy population of around four million. The Irish diet now includes more than just the potato, although spuds are still a popular part of many meals. Ireland is known for its stews and other dishes made from beef, lamb, and pork, often accompanied by cabbage, onions, carrots, and thick breads. Most Irish foods are warm, comforting, and perfect to eat on wet and chilly days. The Irish also pass time on rainy days with music, often played on the traditional harp, fiddle, and bagpipes. They also enjoy dances, including the Irish jig, which has an interesting history. When Ireland fell under British rule, the British outlawed everything traditionally Irish. This meant that performing dances to Irish music was illegal.

Some bagpipers were even arrested! The Irish cherished their own music and dances, and so they began to perform them in secret. Irish dance masters traveled around the countryside, residing with different families and teaching their dances to many Irish citizens so that the dances would not be forgotten. They danced the jig in farm fields, on roads, at secret schools, and even in kitchens on tabletops. They invented new dance steps and sometimes participated in secret dance competitions, where the dance master who knew the most steps would win. Sometimes a dancer's skill was tested when he was asked to perform on top of a wobbly barrel.

Ireland is also known for its castles, many of which can be found in Dublin, the country's capital city. Citizens and tourists can walk through their magnificent gardens and explore the majestic castles, many of which still have furniture and other antique items belonging to their former residents. The Dublin Castle was built in the early 1200s and was home to many British leaders until as recently as 1922. The Malahide Castle, located on the seaside, is even older than the Dublin Castle and was home to members of the same family for almost 800 years. Other historic buildings in the capital city include large government buildings, an ancient prison that is no longer used, churches (called abbeys), and former homes of famous Irish writers and other artists.

Another association with Ireland is the country's national holiday, Saint Patrick's Day. Saint Patrick was born around the year 385 CE, and at this time, the Irish were a pagan people, meaning that they didn't belong to an established religion such as Christianity, Judaism, or Islam. Saint Patrick was a pagan until he reached the age of sixteen when he decided to become a Christian. He then became a bishop and set out to spread Christianity throughout Ireland, building churches and schools where the religion could be taught. He spread Christianity for thirty years before his death, and two hundred years after he started, most of Ireland was Christian. A famous story of Irish folklore tells how Saint Patrick gave a sermon from a hillside and drove all the snakes from Ireland, which is intended to explain why no snakes exist in Ireland today. Although snakes probably never lived in Ireland, the story likely represents the banishment of paganism from the country.

FORM OPINIONS AND DRAW CONCLUSIONS | **Lesson 4**

Saint Patrick's Day is celebrated on March 17th because it is said that this was the date of Saint Patrick's death. This Irish national holiday was once solely a religious holiday, but it has expanded to include festivities such as parades, fireworks, concerts, and much more. Interestingly, it is said that the first Saint Patrick's Day parade took place in 1700s America when Irish soldiers marched through New York City to celebrate the patron saint of Ireland. Today, although it is Ireland's national holiday, Saint Patrick's Day is also celebrated in America, Canada, Australia, Russia, Japan, and other places around the world.

 Questions

1. Which experience would BEST help you learn about Ireland?

    A. going to a St. Patrick's Day parade
    B. talking to a relative from Ireland
    C. learning how to do the Irish jig
    D. reading an Irish cookbook

 Tip
Select the answer choice that would help you learn many different things about Ireland, instead of only one aspect.

2. Which of the following contributed MOST to the population growth in Ireland after the potato famine?

    A. refusing to rent from British landlords
    B. learning more about the weather
    C. learning how to grow different kinds of food
    D. leaving the country to search for food

 Tip
Read the paragraph after the paragraph that discusses the famine. What does the author say about the Irish diet?

Lesson 4 **FORM OPINIONS AND DRAW CONCLUSIONS**

3.   The author of the article informs readers about many different aspects of Ireland.

- If you were to travel to Ireland, what do you think you would like most?
- What part of Irish culture would you like to learn more about?

Use details and information from the story in your answer.

Check your answers on the next page. Read the explanation after each answer.

Passage 4: "The Emerald Isle"

 Answers

1. **B** Talking to a relative from Ireland would probably be the best way to learn more about Ireland. The other answer choices focus on only one aspect of Ireland, such as dancing or food.

2. **C** The author says that after the famine, the Irish diet expanded to include foods other than potatoes. Therefore, answer choice C is the best answer.

3. **Sample answer:** If I were to travel to Ireland I think I would appreciate the scenery the most. The article says that it rains often in Ireland and the landscape is a lush green. I think this would be beautiful. I would like to learn more about the castles in Ireland. They sound as if they're very beautiful and an important part of Ireland's history.

Lesson 5: Interpretation of Textual Conventions and Literary Elements

This lesson covers the following skill for reading (3.1: E.1, G.8, G.9, G.16, and G.21): Interpretation of textual conventions and literary elements.

For the reading section of this test, questions for these skills may be either multiple-choice or open-ended questions. For open-ended questions, you will write out your answers in your answer booklet. This essay is longer than an open-ended question. You will do some prewriting before writing this essay. You will learn more about this portion of the test in **Part 2: Writing, Revising, and Viewing**.

How do you interpret textual conventions and literary elements?

Several different types of questions you'll see on the ASK relate to literature. Questions about narrative (fictional) passages might ask you to identify the conflict or the tone of a short story. They might ask about the setting of literature. They might also ask you about characters' motivations, or why the characters do the things that they do.

Questions assessing this skill might also ask you to identify or analyze writing conventions (how the author uses writing to convey meaning). For example, a question might ask you why an author repeats a certain idea or why an author uses a specific technique, such as flashback.

Activity

Read the following fable. How does the fox's behavior in the beginning impact other events later in the story? How could the fox have avoided the conflict?

The Fox and the Stork

(adapted from Aesop's Fables)

Once upon a time, a fox and a stork were friends. The fox invited the stork to dinner. The fox loved soup, so he placed soup in two shallow bowls on the table. The fox ate his soup, but the stork could not eat hers. She tried and tried, but could not get the soup out of the shallow bowl with her long, pointed beak. At first, the stork tried to be polite to the fox, just in case he did not realize his error. However, the stork eventually became very hungry, and then became angry. "I'm sorry the soup is not to your liking," the fox said.

"Oh, do not apologize," said the stork. "I hope you will return this visit and dine with me soon."

So the two chose a day and the fox visited the stork for dinner. The stork also served delicious soup, but she served it in two long-necked jars with narrow mouths. The fox could not get the soup out of the jar, while the stork had no problem doing so. "I will not apologize for dinner," said the stork. "One bad turn deserves another."

_____

_____

_____

_____

Passage 1

Read the following passage and answer the questions that follow.

Bitter Competition

Sarah Kowalski and Rosa Lee had been best friends since they were very young. They grew up in the same neighborhood, played in the same playgrounds, and attended the same school. However, there was a unique component to their friendship—they found themselves constantly in competition.

For a while, the competitiveness enhanced their friendship. They enjoyed playing chess to determine which of them could outsmart and outmaneuver the other. Whenever they participated in sports, they played on opposing teams in order to determine who could pitch, catch, or throw with the greatest skill. In the classroom they routinely compared their test scores and strived to outdo one another every time a math or science test rolled around.

The Lee and Kowalski families were pleased because the competition appeared to make their daughters thrive. Both girls were honor-roll students who excelled in athletics. What the families failed to comprehend was that both Sarah and Rosa often got frustrated by their inability to get an upper hand in their contests and that this frustration was beginning to take its toll on their friendship.

One morning, the girls discovered that there was an important midterm exam approaching in their Algebra I class. Sarah was distressed about that because algebra was her weak spot. She just couldn't grasp the concept of replacing numbers with letters. Worst of all, she knew that Rosa was proficient at algebra and might take an overwhelming lead in their contests. Sarah was determined to put an end to Rosa's winning streak.

Sarah began studying diligently for the algebra exam a week in advance. Although she felt resolved, she was still having difficulty with the material and the extra pressure of the competition was driving her crazy. The night before the exam, Sarah disappeared into her room to try to memorize all she could. She recited, "The FOIL method—multiply the First term, then the Outer, then the Inner, then the Last. First, Outer, Inner, Last—that spells FOIL." Then she closed the book and recited it from memory. She was thrilled that she had absorbed some information, and thought maybe her cause wasn't so hopeless after all.

The next morning, Sarah watched anxiously as her algebra teacher passed out the exam. She wanted to get the paper in her hands as soon as possible. Otherwise, she feared, she would forget what she had memorized. As soon as the exam was on her desk, she hunched over it and began scanning it—most of the questions dealt with the FOIL method, as she had anticipated. As soon as she began to write, though, her mind went blank. She couldn't recollect what the letters in FOIL represented.

Sarah tried to stay relaxed, but then she glanced over at Rosa, who was jotting down numbers and equations rapidly. Rosa was flying through the exam! Seeing this made Sarah even more uncomfortable and made her memory even worse. Did the F in FOIL stand for "front," "fraction," "first," "furthest"—or "failure"?

Before she knew it, the class was over and she had no alternative but to submit the exam with only a few questions answered. The next day she was disappointed, but not surprised, to see that she had failed the exam miserably. After class, Rosa approached her, smiling broadly. "I got a 97 on that one. What a piece of cake!"

Suddenly Sarah felt furious, and vented her frustration on Rosa. "So what? Big deal—you're better at math than I am and you got a better grade. Well, who cares?"

Rosa was speechless.

"I got a 46," Sarah announced. "And it's partially your fault. I was looking at you writing so quickly and I was so worried about our stupid competitions that I couldn't even remember what FOIL stands for."

Rosa's eyes filled with tears. "Sarah, I'm really sorry," she said, suddenly awakening to the realization that she and Sarah were now more competitors than friends. "I feel awful about your grade, really I do. I'm certain we could work this problem out if we discuss it maturely." Despite Rosa's plea, Sarah spun around and stormed away.

Later in the day, Rosa approached Sarah again. "Sarah, please forgive me. I'm sorry I didn't see how upset you were. You're my best friend—I don't know what I would do without you," she pleaded.

Sarah smiled, though it was a dejected smile. It seemed that she had redirected her anger at herself. "It's okay, Rosa," she said. "Don't worry about it. I'm just a really poor student, and you're better than me, that's all."

"No, I'm not!" Rosa countered. "You just messed up this one time. How about we study for the next test together? This way we'll both be winners—and no more contests. If I lose your friendship, I will be the biggest loser ever!"

Sarah hugged Rosa and accepted Rosa's offer to study together. They promised that from now on they would help each other instead of competing against each other.

 Questions

1. Why does Sarah fail her algebra test?

   _____

   _____

2. What is the conflict in the story?

   _____

   _____

3. How does Sarah and Rosa's friendship change throughout the story?

   _____

   _____

   _____

   _____

Check your answers on the next page.

Passage 1: "Bitter Competition"

 Answers

1. **Sample answer:** Sarah fails her algebra test because she becomes so nervous that, when she sees Rosa quickly completing the test, she can't remember what FOIL stands for.

2. **Sample answer:** The conflict in the story occurs when Sarah lashes out at Rosa and no longer wants to be her friend. The competition between the girls had gotten out of hand by this point in the story.

3. **Sample answer:** In the beginning of the story, the girls are friends but they are also in competition with each other regarding school and sports. After Sarah fails her test and Rosa feels badly, they decide to stop competing and help each other. They are no longer competitors, just friends.

Passage 2

Read the following passage and answer the questions that follow.

A Day to Remember

Charissa brushed her long brown hair and inspected her reflection in the mirror perched on her bureau. The night before, she had stared into her closet for hours, sifting through piles of clothing, searching for the perfect outfit for the special event. She finally decided on a new khaki skirt, a chocolate brown sweater, and a new pair of boots, and she positioned everything on the overstuffed armchair in the corner of her room so her clothing would remain wrinkle-free. After all, not every day was her fourteenth birthday, and Charissa wanted to make sure it was a memorable occasion—a day that she would cherish forever.

When she heard a knock on her bedroom door, Charissa readied herself for her family's traditional birthday serenade—an off-key version of "Happy Birthday," including a colorfully frosted cupcake and burning candle. Charissa opened the door slowly and cracked a slightly embarrassed smile, but to her dismay, she saw only her mother standing outside of her door, holding a basket of clean, unfolded laundry instead of a birthday cupcake covered in frosting and dotted with sprinkles.

"Sorry, dear, but I need an empty clothesbasket," she chirped as she hurriedly dumped the laundry on Charissa's bed and turned toward the stairs, stopping to give Charissa a quick peck on the cheek. "You have five minutes before I officially close the kitchen, so you better hurry and get some breakfast," she bellowed as she descended the stairs.

Charissa's disbelief that her mother had forgotten her fourteenth birthday slowly washed over her, and she lingered in her room until she had accepted the depressing fact. She miserably grabbed her backpack and purse and trudged to the kitchen, following the aroma of burnt toast and strong coffee that was filtering down the hallway. In the kitchen, Charissa's mother was at the counter busily wrapping peanut butter-and-jelly sandwiches in plastic and packing lunchboxes with carrot sticks and juice boxes. Charissa's father barely glanced up from the newspaper as he mumbled a muffled greeting into his coffee cup. Charissa's younger brother, Nicky, sat on a stool at the counter, gleefully spinning himself in circles while his cereal sat, soggy and untouched, in a bear-shaped bowl. No one mentioned her birthday or commented on her special outfit or her perfect birthday hairdo. In fact, they barely noticed that she had entered the room.

Charissa glanced out the window and caught a glimpse of the school bus rounding the corner, so she swiftly donned her thick wool jacket, grabbed her lunchbox and an orange from a bowl on the table, and disappeared out the door, barely muttering a good-bye to her parents. While she considered it despicable that her family had forgotten her birthday, she knew her friends would remember, and at least this would brighten her day.

INTERPRETATION OF LITERARY ELEMENTS **Lesson 5**

When Charissa stepped off the bus in front of her school, she was pleased to see that her friends had already arrived. They stood in a small huddle, talking and laughing as Charissa approached, their breath creating puffs of steam in the frosty December air. "Hey, Charissa, did you study for the history exam today?" asked Melinda, frantically flipping through several pages of crumpled, messy notes. "I can't seem to find my notes on the Articles of Confederation."

Charissa reached into her neatly organized backpack for her blue history binder while her friends continued to chatter about some television show they had watched the previous night. Charissa handed the notebook to Melinda, who quickly flipped to the pages she needed. Charissa's friend Polly looked at her curiously. *Oh, this is it*, thought Charissa, *someone's finally going to ask me if I feel more mature, more grown-up, and more special now that I'm fourteen.* However, instead of questioning Charissa, Polly quickly responded to a comment from someone else in the group. Charissa grumbled something to her friends about class and jetted off to conceal her obvious disappointment. First her family, and then her best friends, had forgotten her fourteenth birthday—it was turning out to be the most horrible birthday ever!

Throughout the day, Charissa continually expected to hear the words "Happy Birthday" from any-one—friends, classmates, teachers, the principal, even the cafeteria workers, but no one seemed to remember. By the afternoon, her depression affected her concentration and she was incapable of focus-ing on Ms. Washington's science lecture about the atmosphere. On the bus ride home, Charissa blinked back tears as she thought of all the people who were supposed to care about her—the very same people who had forgotten this important day.

When the bus arrived at Charissa's house, she gathered her belongings and began the long trek up her driveway. As she ascended the front steps to her house her mother came out on the porch to meet her. Charissa looked at her with tear-filled eyes and her mother gently put her arm around Charissa's shoulders.

"Charissa, I want to apologize," she said quietly as they planted themselves on the frigid concrete steps and gazed across the sprawling, snow-covered lawn. "Your father and I were heartbroken when we realized that we had forgotten your birthday, and that you missed out on our family tradition. You poor thing, you must have felt wretched all day."

Charissa nodded, wiping her eyes with her sleeve, and described how horrible it felt that no one— not her parents, friends, or teachers—had acknowledged her birthday, and that she hadn't received a sin-gle slice of cake, dollop of ice cream, or birthday gift from anyone. Her careful preparations for a special and memorable fourteenth birthday had been wasted. Charissa's mother listened patiently and embraced her daughter securely as Charissa voiced her complaints about her horrible birthday.

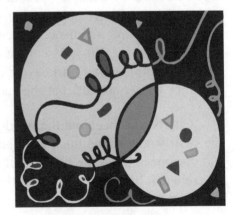

"Come inside and I'll cook a special birthday dinner," her mother said as she turned the doorknob and stepped into the house, Charissa close behind. They entered the foyer, and as Charissa turned the corner and walked into the living room, she was greeted with a roomful of vibrant balloons and streamers, a huge banner that read "Happy 14th Birthday!" and a booming chorus of "SURPRISE!"

 Questions

1. What is Charissa's biggest problem in the story?

    A. She does not know what to wear on her birthday.
    B. Her mother does not give her a cupcake and a candle.
    C. Everyone she knows seems to have forgotten her birthday.
    D. She has trouble concentrating in science class.

 Tip

Think about the major conflict in the story. Which problem is emphasized?

2. Where does the beginning of the story take place?

    A. in Charissa's bedroom
    B. in Charissa's kitchen
    C. outside of a school
    D. on a school bus

 Tip

Reread the first paragraph of the story. Where is Charissa?

3. What happens at the end of the story that solves Charissa's problem?

    A. Her family throws her a party.
    B. Her mother apologizes to her.
    C. She tells her mother what happened.
    D. She smiles and hugs her mother.

 Tip

Think about Charissa's problem and what happens at the end of the story.

Check your answers on the next page.

Passage 2: "A Day to Remember"

 Answers

1. C   While all of these answer choices are problems Charissa faces during the day, only answer choice C tells her biggest problem.

2. A   Charissa is in her bedroom getting dressed in the beginning of the story. Therefore, answer choice A is correct.

3. A   Charissa's problem is solved when she realizes that her family and friends have thrown her a surprise party and that they hadn't forgotten her birthday after all.

Passage 3

Read the following passage and answer the questions that follow.

Mr. Salazar

Donning a new shirt and shorts and with his book bag on his back, Seth proceeded toward the bus stop. *The first day of school is always a blast*, Seth thought. He was eagerly anticipating seeing some of his friends that he wasn't able to touch base with over summer vacation while he worked with his grandfather on his farm.

Seth felt certain that eighth grade was going to be his best year ever. As one of the oldest students, he knew nearly everyone in the school. He was going to be on the varsity basketball team and might even be chosen as a starter. The best part, however, would be having Mr. Jordan as his homeroom teacher.

Mr. Jordan had been Seth's English teacher for several years and Seth really enjoyed his classes, mainly because Mr. Jordan had an incredible sense of humor and managed to make learning great fun. After the class had read a new short story or novel, he would match students to characters and have the students act out a chapter or two. While at first Seth thought this would be extremely corny and contemplated outright refusing to comply with it, he changed his mind when Mr. Jordan assigned him the role of an old woman in one of Flannery O'Connor's short stories. Seth tried in vain to raise his deep voice so it resembled an old woman's, but all he managed to do was squeak—and make his classmates crack up with riotous laughter. Then Mr. Jordan assigned Seth's friend Charlie the part of a desk, which required Charlie to be quiet, a seemingly impossible task. Once everyone had their parts, they managed to get through it without laughing too loudly. Mr. Jordan discussed character motivation by asking each student (except Charlie) what made their character do the things that he or she did. In Seth's perception, Mr. Jordan was in the running for one of the world's greatest teachers.

This is why Seth was completely distraught to discover another man standing in front of Mr. Jordan's desk. "Who's *that*?" he asked his friend Ashley. "And why is he in Mr. Jordan's classroom leaning on his desk?" Ashley shook her head and told Seth she had no clue. The man was much younger than Mr. Jordan and, even though he hunched his shoulders and leaned forward slightly, he was much taller—too tall, in Seth's opinion. The man slipped his hands into his pockets nervously and smiled an awkward, crooked smile. When Seth's eyes met his, he nodded, but Seth was too bewildered to respond.

When everyone entered the room, the man introduced himself as Mr. Salazar. "Are you a substitute?" called out someone from the back of class.

Mr. Salazar shook his head negatively. "Mr. Jordan and his wife relocated to Philadelphia about a month ago, and I have been bestowed the honor of being your teacher this year."

While some students clapped and welcomed Mr. Salazar, Seth was too stunned to respond. His whole mood was stifled by the thought: *No more Mr. Jordan?* That meant no more funny plays, no joking around in class—learning would no longer be enjoyable. This man did not resemble Mr. Jordan in the slightest. He looked serious, nervous, and much too young to be a teacher. "Is this the first class you've ever taught?" Seth inquired.

INTERPRETATION OF LITERARY ELEMENTS   **Lesson 5**

Mr. Salazar laughed. "Yes," he replied. "I graduated college last May, but I student-taught during my last year and learned a great deal. I'm going to teach you many new and interesting things and we're going to have lots of fun learning."

Yeah right, Seth thought. *This is going to ruin everything.*

Seth and his friend Charlie made a beeline for the basketball court at recess. Seth was surprised to see Mr. Salazar on the court dribbling a basketball. His lanky frame moved surprisingly swiftly as she approached the hoop. He reached up and gently shot the ball—*swish!* Mr. Salazar stopped when he saw them. "Hey boys, would you like to play?" he inquired.

Seth and Charlie approached him as two more boys walked onto the court. "You play basketball?" Seth asked him, surprised that someone who seemed so awkward and gangly would be involved in athletics.

"You bet!" replied Mr. Salazar enthusiastically. "I played in both high school and college."

Seth caught the rebound and tried unsuccessfully to pass by Mr. Salazar. Seth chuckled. "For a too-tall dude, you can really move," he joked. Mr. Salazar knocked the ball away from Seth and sunk it into the hoop. A crowd of students gathered around the court to watch Mr. Salazar's incredible skills. Seth's classmates attempted to defeat him in a lopsided four-on-one match, but it was to no avail. Exhausted, Seth plopped down on the side of the court. "You're so tall, no one can beat you," Seth said.

"Nah," Mr. Salazar replied and sunk yet another basket without breaking a sweat. "Size doesn't have all that much to do with it. Some of the best players on my college team were only average height, if not smaller. It's how you maneuver that makes the difference."

"You are really awesome," Seth said. "You are *really* awesome. Could you teach us to move like that?"

"Sure!" said Mr. Salazar. "I'm going to teach you lots of things—and not just about basketball. We're going to start a new novel in English today called *Dogsong.* Have you ever heard of it?"

Dogsong was written by Gary Paulsen, Seth's favorite author. Seth told Mr. Salazar about the other books he had read by Paulsen. When the bell rang ending recess, Seth headed back to class excited for the first time since he'd arrived at school. Maybe his fears weren't warranted and things weren't so bad after all.

Questions

1. Seth's feelings change throughout the story. Compare how he feels when he first sees Mr. Salazar to how he feels at the end of the story. What happened to cause his feelings to change?

    Use details from the story to support your answer.

    _____

    _____

    _____

    _____

    _____

Tip
Reread the story. Note Seth's feelings as the story progresses. What does Mr. Salazar do that causes Seth to admire him?

2. What did Seth like about Mr. Jordan?

    A. He made learning fun.
    B. He was extremely tall.
    C. He knew how to play basketball.
    D. He liked to read books by Gary Paulsen.

Tip
Look back to the beginning of the story. What does Mr. Jordan do that makes Seth happy?

3.   What is Seth's main conflict in the story?

    A.   Mr. Salazar is too tall.
    B.   Mr. Jordan has moved away.
    C.   Seth wants to play basketball.
    D.   Seth is starting the eighth grade.

Tip

Remember that the conflict is the biggest problem in the story. What is Seth's biggest problem?

4.   Why does the author repeat the same sentence in paragraph 14?

    A.   to emphasize that Seth is impressed with Mr. Salazar
    B.   to show that Seth likes being around Mr. Salazar
    C.   to show that Seth has listened carefully to Mr. Salazar
    D.   to emphasize that Seth is trying to get Mr. Salazar's attention

Tip

Reread paragraph 14. Why would Seth say the same thing twice?

Check your answers on the next page. Read the explanation after each answer choice.

Passage 3: "Mr. Salazar"

 Answers

1. Your answer should compare how Seth feels when he first sees Mr. Salazar to how he feels at the end of the story and indicate what made his feelings change.

    Sample answer:

    Seth starts out very excited about the start of the school year because he will have his favorite teacher, Mr. Jordan, as homeroom teacher. He is surprised to discover another man in Mr. Jordan's classroom. When he learns that this man is taking Mr. Jordan's place, he does not think much of him. Mr. Salazar is young and awkward and Seth does not think he will be any good. Seth gets to know the new teacher better when he plays basketball with him, however, and his skill impresses Seth. Then Mr. Salazar tells Seth they are going to read a book by Gary Paulsen, Seth's favorite author. Seth's mood improves and he feels more willing to give Mr. Salazar a chance.

2. A   In the beginning of the story, Seth says that Mr. Jordan was a great deal of fun and a good teacher. Answer choice A is correct.

3. B   The main conflict in this story is that Mr. Jordan has moved away, which means that Seth has a new teacher. Answer choice B is the best answer.

Passage 4

Read the passage and answer the questions that follow.

The Adventures of Gilgamesh

The people of Babylonia felt that their king, Gilgamesh, was a mixed blessing. On one hand, he was the mightiest and most influential king in the world. He was a hero of many battles, a son of the gods, and a man of endless intelligence and insight. He had envisioned and built the city of Uruk, a marvel of architecture with towering gates and brilliantly designed buildings. In the center of Uruk was a lapis lazuli, a gemstone with the proportions of a boulder. Carved into this stone were the chronicles of Gilgamesh's many adventures. Reading them over, nobody could deny that he had earned his fame.

However, Gilgamesh was also arrogant and brash, and frequently neglected the concerns of his people in order to concentrate on himself. On occasion he was downright oppressive, and when he began to interfere in citizens' marriages, the people decided something had to be done. They flocked to the temple and prayed to their chief god, Anu, pleading with him to confront Gilgamesh and end his exploitation. Their prayers were answered with silence, though, and the people left the temple disappointedly.

The next day, a hunter named Shuja headed into the forests outside the city in search of game. As soon as he stepped into the thick, shadowy woods, he heard an animal roar that he did not recognize. It resembled a horrifying combination of the growls, hoots, whistles, and barks of a dozen different species. He heard it again, and it was closer this time. Before he could evacuate, he found himself face-to-face with a hulking wild man surrounded by a team of vicious animals.

An hour later, an exhausted Shuja returned to the city. He looked so ragged and terrified that a crowd gathered around him, inquiring what troubles had befallen him. "I encountered a wild man in the forest, training animals for warfare," Shuja explained. "His name was Enkidu, and he said Anu had dispatched him to dethrone King Gilgamesh."

A worried murmur passed through the crowd. What would happen if such a menacing creature attacked Uruk, they wondered. The prospect was even less pleasant than the prospect of Gilgamesh's continued oppression. They realized they needed to stop Enkidu, but how could they negotiate with an animal-like man? Some thought they should fight; some thought they should flee. Some thought they should surrender to the creature and some believed they could reason with it. Nobody could agree on a course of action.

"Stop this quarreling; I'll solve this predicament," announced Shamhat, one of the most beautiful women in Uruk. The next morning she left the city's protective walls and proceeded into the forest in search of Enkidu. She found him at a watering hole where he and his supporters had bivouacked. Shamhat approached him, and he could sense that she was not motivated by apprehension or hostility. This caught Enkidu off guard.

Shamhat addressed Enkidu with kindness and compassion, and he responded in a similarly civil manner. They spent the day together and, the next morning, she led him into Uruk as a friend, not an enemy. The people gathered around them and celebrated the cessation of his threat. Enkidu, though disoriented by the new environment, came to love the beauty, companionship, and sophistication he encountered inside the city walls. Taking up residence with some shepherds, Enkidu learned how to behave like a civilized human being.

Meanwhile, Gilgamesh had been having visions of powerful, mysterious newcomers trespassing upon his land. It was therefore no surprise to him to learn of Enkidu's presence in Uruk. Gilgamesh consulted with his mother, who advised him to embrace this newcomer as a friend, because together they were destined for great accomplishments.

"*What does she know?*" Gilgamesh thought bitterly. "*I would not degrade myself by accepting some wild man as a companion.*"

And so Gilgamesh continued his oppression of the people. During a marriage celebration, Gilgamesh interfered again. He was jealous of the groom and intended to kidnap the bride. He believed he was justified in doing so because he was the ruler of Uruk, and he was comfortable with the knowledge that nobody would challenge him. But he'd forgotten about the newcomer, Enkidu, who suddenly appeared in the king's doorway and refused to allow him to break up the wedding.

"How dare you exploit your people for your own gain?" demanded Enkidu.

"How dare you question my decisions?" roared Gilgamesh, lunging forward to attack his challenger.

The two combatants struggled for hours, their powers equally balanced. Finally, Gilgamesh was able to secure an advantage in the battle, and raised a sword high over Enkidu. Instead of bringing the sword slashing down, though, he paused and then slowly lowered the weapon.

"You are a worthy opponent," he admitted, "and I was wrong to belittle you. I see the wisdom in your challenge, and I will not spoil the wedding." Gilgamesh helped Enkidu to his feet, and then they shook hands. "I think my mother was right. If you and I work together, we can accomplish great things for the people of Uruk."

Gilgamesh and Enkidu became fast friends.

 Questions

1. Why were the people of Babylon upset with King Gilgamesh?

   A. He forbade them to pray to Anu.
   B. He listened to his mother's advice.
   C. He made friends with a wild man.
   D. He interfered in wedding ceremonies.

 Tip
If you don't recall this detail, look back to the beginning of the story.

2. Why didn't Gilgamesh want to make friends with Enkidu?

   A. He was afraid of Enkidu.
   B. His mother warned against it.
   C. He knew Enkidu wanted to be king.
   D. He thought he was better than Enkidu.

 Tip
Think about when Gilgamesh first learned about Enkidu. What was his attitude toward the wild man?

3. Enkidu angered Gilgamesh when he challenged the king's authority.

   ● How did Gilgamesh and Enkidu try to resolve their differences?

   ● Why did Gilgamesh decide to accept Enkidu as his ally?

   Use details and information from the story to support your answer.

Tip

Reread the part of the story where Gilgamesh and Enkidu confront one another at the wedding. How did their fight lead to a friendship?

4. How did Enkidu change after meeting Shamhat?

   A. from noble to selfish
   B. from brave to cowardly
   C. from untamed to mannerly
   D. from peace-loving to warlike

Tip

Think about how Enkidu acted before meeting the beautiful Shamhat, and then how he transformed afterwards.

Check your answers on the next page. Read the explanation after each answer choice.

Passage 4: "The Adventures of Gilgamesh"

 Answers

1. D   Early in the story, the people of Uruk were very upset with King Gilgamesh because he often interfered in the people's wedding ceremonies.

2. D   Although Gilgamesh's mother advised that he make friends with Enkidu, Gilgamesh at first refused to do so. He felt that he was too good to be friends with a wild man like Enkidu.

3.   **Sample answer:** When Enkidu saw the king interfering in the wedding, he became furious. In turn, Gilgamesh was furious because Enkidu, a wild man from the forest, dared to question him. The two men began to fight, and the fight lasted for hours because they were both equally skilled warriors. At long last, Gilgamesh seemed to be winning, and he prepared to strike Enkidu with his sword, But he suddenly realized that Enkidu was a fine warrior who could be a great help to him. He also realized that Enkidu was right to challenge him, and he promised not to interfere with the wedding celebration. Instead of killing Enkidu, Gilgamesh offered his hand in friendship and asked for his help protecting the kingdom of Uruk.

4. C   Before meeting Shamhat, Enkidu ran untamed in the forests with the animals. By showing him kindness, Shamhat helped him transform into a mannerly citizen.

PART 2: Writing and Revising

In this part of this book, you will learn how to write essays and answer open-ended questions. On ASK8, you will be asked to respond to two different types of writing prompts. These are essays for which you should do some prewriting, drafting, and revising. On ASK8, you will be asked to respond to the following writing prompts:

- **Speculate**—You will be asked to respond to a prompt. Often, these questions ask you what "story" the picture is telling. You will have 30 minutes to complete this task.

  OR

- **Analyze/Explain**—You may be asked to read a poem and answer a question about the poem. This type of writing prompt usually makes a statement about the poem and then asks you to respond to the statement. For example, it might say, "In this poem, the reader learns an important lesson. Think about a lesson you have learned. Write an explanation of this lesson and analyze why it was important to you." You will have 30 minutes to complete this task.

- **Persuade**—You will be asked to respond to a writing prompt that gives you a situation by taking a stand and persuading readers to believe as you believe. You might be asked to write a letter to the editor about an issue affecting your community or a letter to the school board about a matter concerning your school. You will have 45 minutes to complete this task.

In addition to completing the writing tasks, you will have to answer some open-ended questions in the Reading sections. Open-ended questions require you to write out your answer instead of choosing the best answer. Your answers to open-ended questions should not be as long as an essay, but they should be well written.

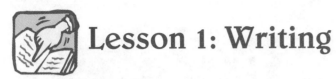

Lesson 1: Writing

This lesson covers the following skills for writing (3.2: A.1, A.3, A.4, A.13, B.8, B.9, D.9, D.15, and D.16): writing a first draft of an essay in response to a writing prompt that:

- Is clear and appropriate for the given prompt
- Has a focus and appropriate supporting details
- Is well organized and has an introduction, transition statements, and a conclusion
- Engages the audience
- Uses varied sentence structure and word choices
- Uses conventions of print and literary forms
- Uses language appropriate to the audience
- Shows understanding of techniques to revise and edit a passage
- Combines information from a variety of sources
- Appropriately addresses the target audience
- Supports and connects your ideas
- Uses a writing format that fits with the given task

Developing Your Essays: The Three Stages of Writing

As you begin to develop your essay, you should follow the three stages of writing: **prewriting**, **drafting**, and **revising**. On ASK8, you may be presented with a picture and asked to speculate about what is happening in the picture. You might be asked to read a poem and analyze or explain the poem. Or you may be given an important issue and asked to explain whether you agree or disagree with the issue. No matter what type of essay you are writing, you should always begin to develop your essay by prewriting.

Prewriting—RECORD Your Ideas

The main purpose of prewriting is to record your ideas. You can do this by brainstorming what you will be writing about in your essay. Start by jotting down ideas and possible angles for your essay. Think about the positive and negative aspects of a topic. Think about the audience for whom you will be writing and the purpose of your writing. Are you writing to entertain readers with a story, give your opinion, or explain something? Once you have determined your central idea, purpose, and audience, write down some supporting material and organize or outline your ideas into a logical sequence.

Suppose your task is to write an essay in support of or against tearing down an old building:

> At the last city council meeting, a local business owner asked the council members for permission to tear down a historic building on Main Street to build a new clothing store in its place. Council members were divided on the issue. Some argued that the building was built before the Civil War and had too much historic value to be destroyed. Others argued that the old building was nothing more than an eyesore and a safety hazard and that a new store would make the downtown area more attractive.
>
> The mayor decided to postpone voting on the issue until she could hear more details about both sides of the issue. How do you feel about tearing down the historic building?
>
> Write an essay giving your opinion on the issue. Use facts and examples to develop your argument.

How would you begin to prepare an essay on this issue? First, you would take a moment to jot down a few notes about the issue. Why is the old building important? What are the benefits of the new store? You would ask yourself how you feel about the issue. Do you disagree with tearing down the building or would you rather have a new clothing store? Once you decide on the angle you want to take in your essay, add some details to support your position. You could create a web to help develop your argument and organize your ideas.

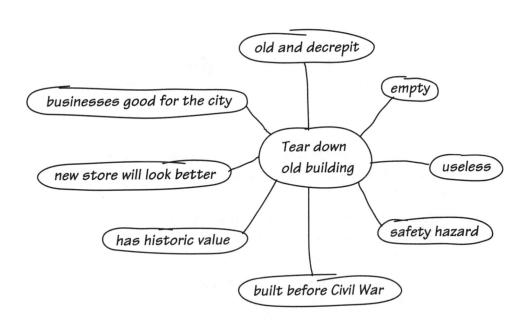

Prewriting— EVALUATE Your Ideas

When you have finished developing your argument, evaluate what you've written. Which ideas will help persuade the reader to share your opinion? Which ideas might weaken your argument? Don't be afraid to eliminate one or more of your ideas.

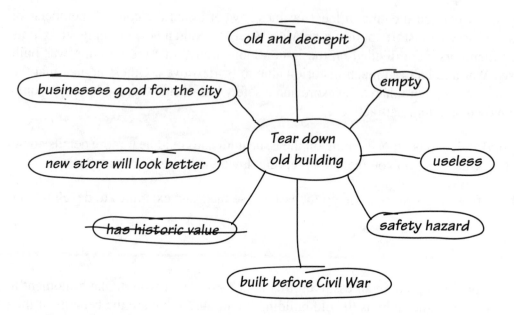

The fact that the building has historic value doesn't support the argument to tear it down. You probably wouldn't want to focus your essay on the historic value of the building if you were trying to convince readers to tear it down.

Prewriting—ORGANIZE Your Ideas

A good essay is organized into three parts:

1. **Introduction**—An essay should always begin with an introduction. The introduction should give readers a good idea of what to expect in the essay and give them a clue as to why you are writing the essay.

2. **Body**—The body of the essay is where you present the main ideas of the essay. Your main ideas, or in this example your main arguments, should be clearly explained. State your main ideas or opinions and support them with details.

3. **Conclusion**—The conclusion should provide a quick summary of your essay and leave the reader with your final word on the issue.

Drafting—Begin Your FIRST DRAFT

In the drafting stage of writing, you will write a rough draft of your work. An important thing to remember when writing your draft is to get your ideas down on paper. In this stage of writing, your writing does not have to be perfect. It is acceptable for the rough draft to have mistakes in grammar, spelling, and punctuation. These mistakes can be changed or fixed later.

Your first draft may look something like this:

I think that replacing the building with a new clothing store is a grate idea. At the last city council meeting a local business owner asked permishon to tear down the old building on Main St. The business owner wants to build a new clothing store in its place. I think city council should vote for this project.

Right now, the old building is full of broke windows. The doors are missing and bats and rats live their. More than anything, the building is an eye sore. A new building of any kind would look better.

Some city council members have argued that the old building is historic. Because it was built before the civil war. But, they fail to mention that the building has is in disrepare. Building a new store will improve the look of the downtown area. Pieces of broken glass and brick could easily fall to the ground and hurt people on the sidewalk the building is just not safe.

Finally, the old building is empty and useless. Bilding a new store in it's place would bring more people and more money into the city. It's taking up a lot of space and it's not being used for anything.

I would like to ask all city council members to think about how wonderful Main St. could look if the unsafe, useless, eyesore of a building was torn down. And replaced with a brand new store.

Revising and Editing—Preparing the FINAL DRAFT

After you write your rough draft, it's time to begin revising and editing your work. Read your rough draft carefully. Look for mistakes in grammar, spelling, punctuation, and capitalization. Look for sentence fragments. Make sure that you have stated your main idea or that you have provided enough supporting details for readers to determine the central theme. Reword sentences or move entire paragraphs to make your writing flow in a clear, logical order. Add more details to make your writing vibrant and exciting.

Editorial Symbols

When you edit your first draft, you will find it helpful to use editorial symbols. These are marks on the page that show how you want your composition to be improved. The most common editorial symbols are

ℒ	This is a delete symbol. It tells you what should be removed from the text.
∧	This is an insert symbol. It tells you what should be added to the text.
⊙	This symbol tells you to add a period.
≡	This mark under a letter means that it should be changed to an uppercase letter.
/	This mark through a letter tells you that it should be changed to a lowercase letter.
⌒	This symbol means that you should delete a word or space and bring the surrounding letters together.

When you have finished revising your first draft, refer to the Writer's Checklist to help perfect your essay. Make sure that your essay hits each point listed in the following Writer's Checklist. Then write the final copy of your work in the answer booklet of your test.

Writer's Checklist

_____ Focus on the main idea of your writing and think about your audience.

_____ Support your main idea with interesting facts and details.

_____ Organize your ideas in a logical sequence that best communicates what you are trying to say.

_____ Vary the length and structure of your sentences.

_____ Know the meanings of the words you choose, and use them correctly.

_____ Check the basics. Make sure your capitalization, punctuation, and spelling are correct.

_____ Use your best handwriting for the final copy of your writing.

_____ Appropriately address the target audience

_____ Support and connect your ideas

The final draft of your essay might look something like this:

At the last city council meeting, a local business owner asked permission to tear down the old building on Main Street and construct a new clothing store in its place. I think that replacing the old, rundown building with a new clothing store is a great idea. I encourage city council to vote in favor of this project.

Some city council members have argued that the old building holds a lot of historic value because it was built before the Civil War. However, they fail to mention that the building has fallen into a state of disrepair. Pieces of broken glass and brick could easily fall to the ground and hurt people on the sidewalk. The building is just not safe.

Replacing the old building with a new store will improve the appearance of the downtown area. Right now, the old building is full of broken windows. The doors are missing and it's home to many bats and rats. More than anything, the building is an eyesore. A new building of any kind would be an improvement.

Finally, the old building is empty and useless. It's taking up a lot of valuable property and not being used for anything. Building a new store in its place would bring more people and more money into the city.

In conclusion, I would like to encourage all city council members to think about how wonderful Main Street could look if an unsafe, useless, eyesore of a building was removed and replaced with a brand new store.

In order to achieve the highest score for your essay, make sure that you use the three stages of writing and the Writer's Checklist. Also, pay attention to the content and organization of your essay, as well as usage, sentence construction, and mechanics.

Content/Organization

As mentioned earlier, your essay should be framed by strong opening and closing ideas. Make sure that you have addressed reasons that your issue is important. Conclude by stating why you feel as you do.

In between the opening and closing of your essay are your main ideas. Make sure that your ideas are clear, and that you have included a variety of main ideas and have not simply stressed the same point multiple times. Your ideas should follow a logical progression, meaning that transition from one main idea to another should not be choppy, but instead should flow easily from one idea to the next. Your ideas should also be supported by details, or reasons why you believe your ideas to be true. Also, be sure that your transitions from the introduction to the body to the conclusion are fluid instead of choppy.

Sentence Construction

Make sure that you follow traditional grammar rules when composing sentences. You should check to make sure that you have placed periods and commas in logical places. Make sure that you vary the length and structure of your sentences. This will help to improve your composition.

Usage

When you revise and edit, make sure that you use correct verb tense and agreement. For example, if you are using past tense verbs to describe something that happened in the past, then make sure that all the verbs describing this past event are in the past tense. Also, look at your pronouns (*I, you, he, she, it, we, they*) to make sure that you have used them correctly. Examine your essay to make sure you have used words that will engage the reader. If you don't like the look or sound of a certain word in your essay, try to replace it with a better one.

Mechanics

Mechanics are the spelling, capitalization, and punctuation in your essay. You are not allowed to use a dictionary during the test, so try to do your best with spelling and capitalization. Using precise spelling, capitalization, and punctuation will make it easier for people to read and understand your essay.

How Essays Are Graded

Your essays will be graded on a six-point (1 through 6) scale. The following scoring rubric outlines how your essay will be scored.

	Inadequate Command	Limited Command	Partial Command	Adequate Command	Strong Command	Superior Command
Score	1	2	3	4	5	6
Content & Organization (see below)	● May lack opening and/or closing	● May lack opening and/or closing	● May lack opening and/or closing	● Generally has opening and/or closing	● Opening and closing	● Opening and closing
	● Minimal response to topic; uncertain focus	● Attempts to focus ● May drift or shift focus	● Usually has single focus	● Single focus	● Single focus ● Sense of unity and coherence ● Key ideas developed	● Single, distinct focus ● Unified and coherent ● Well-developed
	● No planning evident; disorganized	● Attempts organization ● Few, if any, transitions between ideas	● Some lapses or flaws in organization ● May lack some transitions between ideas	● Ideas loosely connected ● Transition evident	● Logical progression of ideas ● Moderately fluent ● Attempts compositional risks	● Logical progression of ideas ● Fluent, cohesive ● Compositional risks successful
	● Details random, inappropriate, or barely apparent	● Details lack elaboration, i.e., highlight paper	● Repetitious details ● Several unelaborated details	● Uneven development of details	● Details appropriate and varied	● Details effective, vivid, explicit, and/or pertinent

	Inadequate Command	Limited Command	Partial Command	Adequate Command	Strong Command	Superior Command
Score	1	2	3	4	5	6
Usage (see below)	• No apparent control • Severe/numerous errors	• Numerous errors	• Errors/patterns of errors may be evident	• Some errors that do not interfere with meaning	• Few errors	• Very few, if any, errors
Sentence Construction (see below)	• Assortment of incomplete and/or incorrect sentences	• Excessive monotony/same structure • Numerous errors	• Little variety in syntax • Some errors	• Some errors that do not interfere with meaning	• Few errors	• Very few, if any, errors
Mechanics (see below)	• Errors so severe they detract from meaning	• Numerous serious errors	• Patterns of errors evident	• No consistent pattern of errors • Some errors that do not interfere with meaning	• Few errors	• Very few, if any, errors

Content & Organization	Usage	Sentence Construction	Mechanics
• Communicates intended message to intended audience • Relates to topic • Opening and closing • Focused • Logical progression of ideas • Transitions • Appropriate details and information	• Tense formation • Subject-verb agreement • Pronouns usage/agreement • Word choice/meaning • Proper modifiers	• Variety of type, structure, and length • Correct construction	• Spelling • Capitalization • Punctuation

SCORE SCALE POINT 1

The response indicates an INADEQUATE COMMAND of written language. The writing samples in this category:

CONTENT/ORGANIZATION	May not have an opening and/or a closing. These papers are on topic and demonstrate at least a minimal attempt to respond to the topic by stating a subject or giving a list of subjects. Some of the lengthier papers are disorganized, making them consistently difficult to follow. Others will relate to the topic but will have an uncertain focus. In these papers the reader has to infer what the focus is. The overriding characteristic of many of these papers is a lack of control with no sense of planning. Details may be random, inappropriate, or barely apparent.
USAGE	May display severe/numerous errors in usage. This includes problems in tense formation, subject-verb agreement, pronoun usage and agreement, word choice, and use of proper modifiers.
SENTENCE CONSTRUCTION	May demonstrate an assortment of grammatically incorrect/incomplete sentences and/or incorrect rhetorical modes. Statements may be either incoherent or unintelligible.
MECHANICS	May display errors in mechanics so severe as to detract from the meaning of the response.

SCORE SCALE POINT 2

This response indicates a LIMITED COMMAND of written language. The writing samples in this category:

CONTENT/ORGANIZATION	May not have an opening and/or a closing. These responses will exhibit an attempt at organization. In other words, there will be some evidence the writer attempted to control the details. The responses relate to the topic, but in some papers, the writer drifts away from the primary focus or abruptly shifts focus. In other papers, there is a single focus, but there are few, if any, transitions, making it difficult to move from idea to idea. Details are presented with little, if any, elaboration—highlight papers.
USAGE	May have numerous problems with usage, but they are not totally out of control.
SENTENCE CONSTRUCTION	May demonstrate excessive monotony in syntax and/or rhetorical modes. There may be numerous errors in sentence construction.
MECHANICS	May display numerous serious errors in mechanics.

SCORE SCALE POINT 3

This response indicates a PARTIAL COMMAND of written language. The writing samples in this category:

CONTENT/ ORGANIZATION	May not have an opening and/or a closing. The responses relate to the topic and usually have a single focus. Some of these papers may drift from the focus or abruptly shift focus; however, in these papers, at least one of the subjects focused upon clearly meets the criteria for a 3. For example: some 3 papers are sparse—they have several details with a little elaboration, but they are organized and controlled; some 3 papers will ramble somewhat, repeating ideas resulting in a lengthy response that otherwise would be sparse; and other 3 papers have elaborated ideas and details, but the writing sample is interrupted by organizational flaws/lapses or by a lack of transition between ideas or between clusters of ideas.
USAGE	May display a pattern(s) of errors in usage.
SENTENCE CONSTRUCTION	May demonstrate little variety in syntax structure and/or rhetorical modes. There may be errors in sentence construction.
MECHANICS	May display a pattern(s) of errors in mechanics.

SCORE SCALE POINT 4

The response indicates an ADEQUATE COMMAND of written language. The writing samples in this category:

CONTENT/ ORGANIZATION	Generally will have an opening and a closing. The responses relate to the topic. They have a single focus and are organized. There is little, if any, difficulty moving from idea to idea. Ideas may ramble somewhat, and clusters of ideas may be loosely connected; however, an over-all progression is apparent. In some papers, development is uneven, consisting of elaborated ideas interspersed with bare, unelaborated details.
USAGE	May display some errors in usage, but no consistent pattern is apparent.
SENTENCE CONSTRUCTION	May demonstrate a generally correct sense of syntax. They avoid excessive monotony in syntax and/or rhetorical modes. There may be a few errors in sentence construction.
MECHANICS	May display some errors in mechanics, but these errors will not constitute a consistent pattern, nor do they interfere with the meaning of the response.

SCORE SCALE POINT 5

This response indicates a STRONG COMMAND of written language. The writing samples in this category:

CONTENT/ ORGANIZATION	Have an opening and a closing. The responses relate to the topic and have a single focus. They are organized and progress logically from beginning to end. The key ideas are developed with appropriate and varied details. Clusters of ideas are strongly connected. Some writers take compositional risks and are, for the most part, successful. Although these papers are flawed, they have a sense of completeness and unity.
USAGE	Have few errors in usage.
SENTENCE CONSTRUCTION	Demonstrate syntactic and verbal sophistication through an effective variety of sentences and/or rhetorical modes. There are few, if any, errors in sentence construction.
MECHANICS	Have few errors in mechanics.

SCORE SCALE POINT 6

This response indicates a SUPERIOR COMMAND of written language. The writing samples in this category:

CONTENT/ ORGANIZATION	Have an opening and closing. The responses relate to the topic and have a single, distinct focus. They are well-developed, complete compositions that are organized and progress logically from beginning to end. A variety of cohesive devices are present, resulting in a fluent response. Many of these writers take compositional risks resulting in highly effective, vivid, explicit, and/or pertinent responses.
USAGE	Have very few, if any, errors in usage.
SENTENCE CONSTRUCTION	Demonstrate syntactic and verbal sophistication through an effective variety of sentences and/or rhetorical modes. There will be very few, if any, errors in sentence construction.
MECHANICS	Have very few, if any, errors in mechanics.

How Open-Ended Responses Are Graded

Some questions in the ASK8 Reading sections require open-ended responses. They are usually about a passage or story that you have read. The answers to open-ended questions are shorter than essays, but they should be written as clearly and completely as possible. Your answers should show that you have a good understanding of the text, and they should include explanations, opinions, and details. In addition, your answers should stay focused on the task.

Open-ended responses are graded on a five-point (0 through 4) scale. The following scoring rubric outlines how your answers will be scored.

Open-Ended Scoring Rubric for Writing

4 points—The student clearly demonstrates an understanding of the task, completes all requirements, and provides an insightful explanation/opinion that links to or extends aspects of the text.

3 points—The student demonstrates an understanding of the task, completes all requirements, and provides some explanation/opinion using situations or ideas from the text as support.

2 points—The student may address all of the requirements, but demonstrates only a partial understanding of the task and uses text incorrectly or with limited success, resulting in an inconsistent or flawed explanation.

1 point—The student demonstrates minimal understanding of the task, does not complete the requirements, and provides only a vague reference to or no use of the text.

0 points—The student's response is irrelevant or off-topic.

In order to achieve a top-score response for an open-ended question, you must show that you understand the task at hand. You must complete all requirements of the task, which means that you must answer the question that has been asked. In addition, you must provide insightful explanations or opinions that link to or extend aspects of the text. This means that you have to think critically and answer the question accordingly.

Lesson 2: Writing to Speculate

This lesson covers the following skills for writing (3.2: A.2, A.3, A.4, A.5, A.6, A.7, A.8, C.5). Viewing a prompt to:

- recognize a theme or central idea.

- look for details in the prompt that develop the theme or central idea.

- interpret the prompt.

- make judgments, form opinions, and draw conclusions.

Writing an essay, in response to a prompt, that:

- responds clearly and stays focused on the prompt.

- selects a focus and supports it with details.

- includes an introduction, appropriate transitions, and a conclusion.

- uses elaboration to engage audience.

- uses a variety of words and details to engage readers.

- uses varied sentence structure and word choice.

- uses conventions of print and literary forms.

- uses language appropriate to the audience.

- combines information from a variety of sources in a written response.

On ASK8, you may be asked to write to speculate. In this case, you will be given a prompt and asked to write a story to explain what is happening or what might happen. For example, you may be presented with a prompt similar to the following:

As you walk down the main street of your town, you notice a crowd of people gathered around a storefront window. Something has caught the attention of several members of the public. Write a story about what has been displayed, the purpose of the display, how people feel about it and so on. Make sure to include specific details about the display in your story.

In order to respond to this question, you must examine the prompt carefully.

- Where were you?

- What did you see?

- Who else is there?

- What stands out about the display?

- What is the item's purpose?

- How does the display make you feel?

- How are people responding?

As you look at the prompt and ask yourself these questions, jot down notes about what you think is happening and organize your ideas. Remember to use the three stages of writing (prewriting, drafting, and revising) as you prepare your story. Also use the Writer's Checklist on **page 127**.

When you are writing to speculate, your answers will be graded using the six-point (1 through 6) rubric provided in Part 2, Lesson 1: Writing. Remember to pay attention to the content and organization of your essay, as well as word usage, sentence construction, and mechanics (spelling, capitalization, and punctuation). Here is an example of a six-point response to the prompt provided at the beginning of this lesson.

Sample Answer:

"What are all those people looking at?" I asked my mother as we hurried toward the candy store. She didn't answer me, but cocked her head with curiosity. She quickly looked over her shoulder to check for traffic and when she saw the road was clear, she rushed us across the street toward the crowd of people.

From a distance, I didn't see anyone I knew. As we got closer, I recognized most of the people from town. There were so many bodies there that we had to shove through to see what was behind the huge window. Finally, I could see through a tiny gap in limbs. What I could make out was a huge banner display and part of a message. Someone way in the back cried out asking what all the hubbub was about.

"The president is coming to visit our town next week for the bicentennial celebration!" As soon as that was announced, there were all sorts of noises from the crowd. Some people started walking away while others crowded tighter around the window. Most of the people seemed really excited. A few folks seemed upset and were mumbling things I couldn't understand. My mother pushed up forward as the crowd thinned out.

Now I had a front row view of the banner and I was eating up every last word. "It says he will be at the August 4th picnic to celebrate the town's 200th birthday. He will judge the chili cook-off with other members of the town council, be a contestant in the pie eating contest and even sit in the dunk tank for an hour! We have got to tell Dad!"

We raced all the way home. A million thoughts were all scrambled up in my head. What was I going to wear? How should I style my hair? What is the president's favorite color? But to me, the most important question of all was whether or not the president likes beans in his chili.

Explanation:

The response stays focused on the prompt, appropriately addresses the audience, follows a single format, and is well organized. There are statements in the opening and closing that are meant to capture the interest of the reader. The writing flows from one idea to the next and there are supportive details to support each main idea. There are some compositional risks, like the use of dialogue, but the grammar, mechanics, and punctuation are otherwise accurate.

Lesson 3: Writing to Analyze/Explain

This lesson covers the following skills for reading and writing (3.2: B.8, D.8, and D.18). Analyzing a poem or text to:

- find a theme or central idea.
- look for details that develop or support the main idea.
- recognize a purpose for reading.
- make judgments, form opinions, and draw conclusions from the text.
- interpret textual conventions and literary elements.

Writing an essay, in response to a writing prompt, that:

- responds clearly and stays focused on the prompt.
- selects a focus and supports it with details.
- includes an introduction, appropriate transitions, and a conclusion.
- uses elaboration to engage the audience.
- uses a variety of words and details to engage readers.
- uses varied sentence structure and word choice.
- uses conventions of print and literary forms.
- uses language appropriate to the audience.
- combines information from a variety of sources in a written response.

On ASK8, you might be asked to write to analyze or explain. One way you may be assessed in this category is that you will be asked to read a quotation and respond to it. The prompts for this type of writing usually ask you to relate the quote to your life. The following is an example of the kind of quotation and prompt that you may face on this part of the test.

Prompt: As part of an assignment for your Language Arts class, your teacher has asked you to explain how the following quotation relates to your personal experiences:

"If at first you don't succeed, try, try again."

Thomas H. Palmer

Write an essay where you explain how this quote relates to your life. Make sure you use details and examples in your response.

The following is an example of a six-point response to the prompt.

If you're like me, you don't always succeed the first time you try something. I have learned that you have to stick with things if you want to get better even if you have trouble getting started. A few years ago, I was ready to give up on playing an instrument because I couldn't master it right away. Luckily, my determination triumphed and I was able to jump the hurdles I faced. It all started when I was in fifth grade. My favorite uncle was in a band and played the electric guitar. The sound that came from that guitar was so beautiful. I was immediately entranced by the instrument and made it my goal to learn how to play what I had just heard. I told my uncle how impressed I was and he told me he would give me some lessons.

One week later, I arrived at my uncle's house eager and ready to make some sweet music on the electric guitar. My uncle strapped on his guitar and gave me one of his spares to use. He plugged both our guitars into an amplifier and showed me how to position my fingers on the fret board. Once I had my fingers in the right spot, he directed me on how to strum the strings with my right hand. The sound that rang out was awkward and piercing, not at all melodic like the sounds my uncle produced. The amplifier fizzled and crackled and sounded like it was going to break. I was immediately discouraged. I went home and swore I'd never pick up a guitar again.

A few days later, my uncle called to ask me why I hadn't come back for another lesson. When I told him it was too tough, he laughed at me and told me that the guitar is one of the most difficult instruments to learn, but also one of the most rewarding to play. He said that he wanted me to stick it out for six months. If I didn't love playing after that, I could quit. He was right about it being really difficult, but I stayed with it for those six months.

Well, here we are one year later and I have to say my uncle was right. I now practice my guitar around four hours a day (even longer on the weekends). My uncle says that soon I'll be good enough to practice with his band. If I would have given up on the guitar after that first lesson, I wouldn't be at this point now. "If at first you don't succeed, try, try again" applies to my life because if I didn't follow that advice, I would have lost out on one of the most enjoyable parts of my life.

Explanation:

The response fulfills all aspects of the prompt and appropriately addresses the audience. The writing is focused, follows a single format, and is well organized. There are very few, if any, mistakes in grammar, mechanics, punctuation, and capitalization. The supportive details and examples are interesting, appropriate and relevant.

Lesson 3   **WRITING TO ANALYZE/EXPLAIN**

Lesson 4: Writing to Persuade

This lesson covers the following skills for writing (3.2: B.8, D.9, D.17, and D.18). Writing a persuasive essay that:

- responds clearly and stays focused on the prompt.

- selects a focus and supports it with details.

- includes an introduction, appropriate transitions, and a conclusion.

- uses elaboration to engage audience.

- uses a variety of words and details to engage readers.

- uses varied sentence structure and word choice.

- uses conventions of print and literary forms.

- uses language appropriate to the audience.

- combines information from a variety of sources in a written response.

On ASK8, you may be asked to write to persuade. You will be presented with an issue that affects your school or community and asked to write a response in support of or against the issue. This type of writing is similar to the example given in Part 2, Lesson 1: Writing, but here we work with another example. The persuasive writing prompt on the test may look something like the following:

> At the last school board meeting, the principal asked permission to cancel all field trips for the remainder of the year in an effort to cut school spending. School board members and parents who attended the meeting were divided on the issue. Some people called field trips "vacations" from school and felt they were unnecessary expenses, while others said that field trips give students a valuable opportunity to learn in a different setting.
>
> The school board decided to table the issue until the next meeting so they could obtain feedback from students on this important issue. What is your opinion of school field trips?
>
> Write a letter to the school board explaining your position on this issue. Use facts and examples to develop your argument.

How would you begin to tackle this issue? First, you would decide whether you were in favor of or against eliminating field trips. Do you agree that field trips are unnecessary, or do you think they are an important part of learning? Once you decide your position on the issue, begin writing some notes that support your opinion. Use the three stages of writing (prewriting, drafting, and revising) that you learned in Part 2, Lesson 1.

When your draft is finished and you've revised and edited your work, remember to check the Writer's Checklist to make sure you've done everything you can to perfect your essay. Pay attention to content and organization, word usage, sentence construction, and mechanics.

The following is an example of a six-point response to the writing prompt in this lesson.

Dear School Board:

School field trips should not be canceled for the rest of the school year. I understand how people might mistake a field trip for a mini-vacation from school. Students get to take a break from the monotony of a school day, get on a bus, and travel to a theater, an art museum, a science center, or a historical site. They get to watch plays, see magnificent works of art, try new inventions, or experience life as it was in the past.

What people seem to forget, however, is that these field trips don't allow us to take a vacation from our education. Rather, field trips allow us to enhance what we've learned in the classroom. While books, chalkboards, and lectures are important, hands-on learning gives students the opportunity to take what they have learned in the classroom and see how it is applied in real life. Why silently read a play when you can see it performed live? Why study paintings in a book when you can look at them in person? Why study pictures of the parts of a flower when you can visit a greenhouse and study the real thing?

Field trips provide us not only with a break from the monotony of a regular school day, but a chance to supplement what we learn in the classroom. It would be a mistake to take away this important part of our education simply to save money.

Sincerely,

Josh Greene

Explanation:

This answer would earn six points because it shows superior command of the English language. The author clearly introduces his argument in the first line of the letter. He clearly understands both points of view in this issue and uses the opposing view make his own argument clear. The essay is well developed and includes a variety of words. Sentences vary in length and construction, and there are few, if any, errors in spelling, punctuation, and capitalization.

Two additional prompts are included here in case you feel the need for any additional practice. Allow yourself 30 minutes for each one. Sample answers follow.

1. Speculative Writing Task—**30** minutes

   Summer vacation was ending fast. You and your friends planned the best last day of vacation ever. Then something happened that made the day even better. Write a story about your plans for the last day of vacation and what happened to make it better.

2. Explanatory Writing Task—**30** minutes

   Consider the importance of the following quotation:

   "Only those who dare to fail greatly can ever achieve greatly."

   —Robert F. Kennedy

   Write an essay explaining what this quotation means to you. Use details, reasons, and examples in your essay.

1. Sample Answer:

> This has been one of the best summers of my life. My friends and I have done so many fun things. We went camping, mountain biking, shopping, swimming, and hiking. We planned a beach party at the end of month to top off our awesome summer. Little did we know what would unfold...
>
> Our main plan was to hit the beach early and claim a huge space so we could set up a volleyball court, space to kick the ball around, a spot to set up the blanket and chairs and an area where we could cook. We had quite a lot of equipment to bring so we all split it up evenly and planned to meet at 7:00am. After a quick stop at the supermarket, we all went home to get ready.

The next morning, we all got there early. I had the grill and started frying up some sausage and bacon for breakfast. Everyone else got to work too and pretty soon it looked like a mini village all around me. We even had a fire pit! I finished cooking breakfast, cleaned up the mess I made and went to enjoy the morning sun. I could tell that this was going to be a good day. The weather was perfect and everyone was in a good mood now that they were full from breakfast.

All of a sudden, I heard several motors approaching from the distance. It took me a minute to realize that they were boat motors and there were a lot of them. We all squinted and put our hands up to block the sun as we gazed down the coastline. Coming toward us was a fleet of speed boats and jet skis. You can imagine how surprised we were when the boats and jet skis started slowing down as they approached us! As the boats pulled up, people started running toward us from the water and we recognized our parents and family. They explained to us that they overheard our plans for the day and wanted to join us and make it better. After we finally grasped what was happening in all the confusion, we got so excited that we couldn't stop laughing and jumping up and down. We didn't think this day *could* get any better.

For the rest of the afternoon, we took turns on the jet skis, water skis, and parasails. We had a huge volleyball tournament which my team won. In the water we used the ball to play water polo, but I got way too tired and had to quit early. After I dried off in the sun, I went to help cook. I couldn't have asked for a better day. The food was amazing, the people were great and the weather was perfect.

When the sun set and the boats left, we let the fire die down. We cleared up our spot and lugged all the gear home. As I sunk into bed that night, I was so exhausted that I could only smile at the amazing day that ended my favorite summer.

Explanation:

The response stays focused on the prompt, appropriately addresses the audience, follows a single format, and is well organized. There are statements in the opening and closing that are meant to capture the interest of the reader. The writing flows from one idea to the next and there are supportive details to support each main idea. There are some compositional risks, like the use of ellipsis (…) but the grammar, mechanics, and punctuation are otherwise accurate.

2. Sample Answer:

Have you ever set out to do something hoping you would fail at it? Have you ever attempted to fail a goal intentionally? I would think that most people generally set out to achieve and reach goals. Kennedy's quote lies at the heart of the reasoning behind attempting to succeed despite apparent obstacles and hurdles.

Risk is a scary thing to some people. One of our natural instincts is to fear unnecessary or heightened risks. However risk is what moves us forward as a people, sometimes by leaps and bounds. The humans that first encountered and worked with fire took a risk and that risk led to significant advancements. Taking risks allows us to explore the unknown with the possibility for failure or success. The fear of that failure cannot stop you from missing out on the benefits of the success.

In my life, I dare to fail and succeed every time I perform a solo in the band. This year is especially tough because I have to compose my own solos and make them fit with the music. Sometimes I do this really well and I can tell because the crowd goes wild. Other times I sound awkward and the crowd's applause holds a tinge of pity. The times I fail miserably are the times I actually learn the most. I hear what didn't work and never do it again. In the end, I know that if I don't try I'll never know if I can. I guess the risk is worth it because I am still in the band.

Overcoming the fear of performing in front of a large audience and playing solos that I came up with myself wasn't easy. Luckily I am the type of person that sets goals for myself and tries to reach them. We can't succeed every time, but if we never try, we can't succeed at all.

Explanation:

The response stays focused on the personal meaning of the quote, appropriately addresses the audience, follows a single format, and is well organized. Questions are asked in the opening paragraph to draw in the reader. There are statements in the opening and closing paragraphs that link the two sections, which helps the reader know the writing is over. The writing focuses on one key idea and uses examples and supportive details to explain.

POSTTEST

This test is also on CD-ROM in our special interactive NJ ASK8 Language Arts Literacy TestWare®. It is highly recommended that you first take this exam on computer. You will then have the additional study features and benefits of enforced timed conditions and instant, accurate scoring. See page viii for guidance on how to get the most out of our NJ ASK8 Language Arts Literacy software.

LANGUAGE ARTS LITERACY POSTTEST PART 1: WRITING TO SPECULATE

For this part of your test, you will be asked to respond to a writing prompt. You will have 30 minutes for this part of the test. Plan and draft your answer on a separate piece of paper. Revise and edit your draft. Then copy your final response into this book. If you finish ahead of time, do not go on to the next part of the test. Wait for your teacher to continue.

WRITING TASK A:
Speculative Prompt (30 minutes)

Your class is going on a really exciting field trip. Write a story about the trip, where you go, what you see, what happens throughout the day, and so on. Make sure you include specific details and use vivid language to make your story interesting to read.

PREWRITING/PLANNING SPACE

When you finish your planning, copy your final response on the lined pages in the answer sheet section at the back of this book.

Be sure to write your draft on the lined pages
in the answer sheet section at the back of this
book. You may check your work on this part only.
DO NOT GO ON TO THE NEXT PAGE

POSTTEST: PART 2
READING: INFORMATIONAL TEXT

In this part of the test, you will read an informational passage and then respond to the multiple-choice and open-ended question that follow it. You will have 30 minutes to read the passage and answer the questions that follow. You may look back at the passage and make notes in your test booklet if you'd like.

The Dragons of Ancient China

Throughout history, people all around the world have been fascinated with dragons. There have been thousands of narratives based on the <u>larger-than-life flying lizards</u> and the lionhearted heroes who interact with them. People across the globe find dragons captivating and compelling, but nowhere have dragons ever been as celebrated as in ancient China.

The ancient Chinese perspective regarding dragons is one you may not expect, however. In America, dragons are typically portrayed as menacing and villainous monsters who crush villages, trample castles, and spew fiery breath at any heroes who dare to challenge them. In ancient China, however, the dragons *were* the heroes. These mythical dragons represented every positive characteristic people admired. They were wise, strong,

compassionate, and beautiful. In many ways, the *Lung*, or dragon, is a symbol of the nation of China.

The ancient Chinese, from peasants to royalty, believed that the Lungs protected their lands and families and assisted them at all times. In fact, the Chinese believed that the people of their nation were descendants of dragons. They believed that Lungs actually created the Chinese people. The ruling classes and royalty in particular felt a connection to the Lungs. Emperors throughout Asia have claimed to have dragons in their families. For instance, Emperor Hirohito, the leader of Japan from 1926 to 1989, believed that the Dragon King of the Sea created his family 2,500 years ago.

According to myth, dragons not only established the royal families of Asia but also continued to advise them. In the 1200s, a king of Cambodia spent hours at a time locked in a golden tower, supposedly <u>conversing</u> with a nine-headed dragon. The greatest emperors were even thought to be dragons themselves! For centuries, people in Japan were not allowed to observe their emperors. People believed this was because the emperors had transformed into Lungs too glorious to look upon.

Today in America, if someone called you "dragon face," you would probably be highly insulted because the phrase suggests ugliness or meanness. If you lived in ancient China, however, if someone called you "dragon face," you would consider it a great compliment. The phrase "dragon face" would suggest that you were extraordinarily beautiful like a dragon. In fact, in ancient China anything compared to a dragon was considered beautiful. For example, dragon-house, dragon-throne, and dragon-land would be considered great compliments. According to ancient Chinese tradition,

GO ON TO THE NEXT PAGE. ➡

there is even a Year of the Dragon during which great prosperity will come to people, especially those born in that year.

Dragons could be seen everywhere in ancient China. They were carved onto musical instruments because people believed they loved music. They were inscribed on books and tablets, because people believed they had a flair for literature. They were even carved outside of temples because people believed they would protect holy places. Thrones, bridges, and swords were all decorated with dragons. The people of ancient Asia wanted dragons to be involved in all aspects of their lives.

These legendary lizards had appearances just as varied as their tasks. They could have skins of any color of the rainbow, though usually they were green or golden. Some sported horns, wings, gigantic teeth, or even catlike whiskers that would help the dragon move around in the deep, dark oceans. For the most part, dragons' body parts resembled the parts of other animals. Many dragons shared characteristics of animals like bulls, frogs, tigers, eagles, and even camels and rabbits. Some dragons began their lives as carp, a type of fish. Other dragons created unique breeds of animals by mating with the creatures of the earth.

People believed that dragons loved to assist them, but only if people appreciated them. If people were unappreciative, a dragon might cause a flood or a drought to punish them. Because of this, the people of ancient Asia went to great lengths to honor dragons. They even had parades during which people would wear elaborate dragon disguises to celebrate the powerful Lungs. These parades are still held today, which shows the lasting influence of this fascinating Chinese tradition.

1. In paragraph 1, what does the author wish to convey with the phrase "larger-than-life flying lizards"?

   A. Dragons are bigger than most other creatures.
   B. Dragons are related to modern flying lizards.
   C. Dragons are fantastic and amazing creatures.
   D. Dragons are found only in ancient stories.

2. What did the body parts of dragons in ancient China usually resemble?

   A. large lizards
   B. other animals
   C. human beings
   D. a type of fish

3. What word BEST describes the author's attitude toward dragons?

   A. fearful
   B. embarrassed
   C. fascinated
   D. superstitious

4. Why did the author write this article?

   A. to describe different types of dragons
   B. to persuade readers to think differently about dragons
   C. to entertain readers with a story about dragons
   D. to inform readers about dragons in ancient China

5. People in Japan believed they were not allowed to see their emperors because they

   A. had turned into dragons.
   B. were reading about dragons.
   C. were spending time with dragons.
   D. were drawing pictures of dragons.

6. As it is used in paragraph 4, what does the word <u>conversing</u> mean?

   A. talking
   B. looking
   C. showing
   D. changing

7. The central idea of the passage is that

   A. all people have revered dragons since ancient times.
   B. people feared dragons because they influenced their lives.
   C. dragons had many influences on ancient Chinese society.
   D. people in ancient China wanted to be like dragons.

8. From the author's point of view, the worldwide appeal of dragon legends is especially interesting because

   A. most legends focus on human characters.
   B. people always realized dragons were imaginary.
   C. the dragons mean different things to different people.
   D. thousands of movies have been made about dragons.

9. What is another word that means the same as the word <u>narratives</u> found in the first paragraph?

   A. Narrator
   B. Lies
   C. Stories
   D. Books

GO ON TO THE NEXT PAGE. ➡

DIRECTIONS FOR QUESTION 10: Write your response in the space provided in the answer sheet section of this book.

10. How did people in ancient China think that dragons influenced their lives?

   Use TWO examples from the passage to support your answer.

END OF PART 2
You may check your work on this part only.
DO NOT GO ON TO THE NEXT PAGE

STOP

POSTTEST: PART 3
READING: NARRATIVE

In this part of the test, you will read a narrative passage and then respond to the multiple-choice and open-ended questions that follow it. You will have 40 minutes for this part of the test. You may look back at the passage and make notes in your test booklet if you like.

INTRODUCTION: This excerpt is from the book Incidents in the Life of a Slave Girl, *in which Harriet Jacobs tells the story of how she struggled for freedom from slavery and a reunion with her children. It is one of the few narratives of slavery written by a woman. In this excerpt, Jacobs is hiding in her Grandmother's attic after escaping from a cruel master named Dr. Flint.*

Excerpt from *Incidents in the Life of a Slave Girl*
by Harriet Jacobs

Much as I despise and detest the class of slave-traders, whom I regard as the vilest wretches on earth, I must do this man the justice to say that he seemed to have some feeling. He took a fancy to William in the jail, and wanted to buy him. When he heard the story of my children, he was willing to aid them in getting out of Dr. Flint's power, even without charging the customary fee.

2 My uncle <u>procured</u> a wagon and carried William and the children back to town. Great was the joy in my grandmother's house! The curtains were closed, and the candles lighted. The happy grandmother cuddled the little ones to her bosom. They hugged her, and kissed her, and clapped their hands, and shouted. She knelt down and poured forth one of her heartfelt prayers of thanksgiving to God. The father was present for a while; and though such a "parental relation" as existed between him and my children takes slight hold of the hearts or consciences of slaveholders, it must be that he experienced some moments of pure joy in witnessing the happiness he had imparted.

I had no share in the rejoicings of that evening.

The events of the day had not come to my knowledge. And now I will tell you something that happened to me; though you will, perhaps, think it illustrates the superstition of slaves. I sat in my usual place on the floor near the window, where I could hear much that was said in the street without being seen. The family had retired for the night, and all was still. I sat there thinking of my children, when I heard a low strain of music. A band of serenaders were under the window, playing "Home, sweet home." I listened till the sounds did not seem like music, but like the moaning of children. It seemed as if my heart would burst. I rose from my sitting posture, and knelt. A streak of moonlight was on the floor before me, and in the midst of it appeared the forms of my two children. They vanished; but I had seen them distinctly. Some will call it a dream, others a vision. I know not how to account for it, but it made a strong impression on my mind, and I felt certain something had happened to my little ones. . . .

At dawn, Betty was up and off to the kitchen. The hours passed on, and the vision of the night kept constantly recurring to my thoughts. After a while I heard the voices of two women in the entry. In one of them I recognized the housemaid. The other said to her, "Did you know Linda Brent's children was sold to the speculator[1] yesterday? They say ole massa Flint was mighty glad to see 'em drove out of town; but they say they've come back again. I 'spect it's all their daddy's doings. They say he's bought William too. Lor! how it will take hold of ole massa Flint! I'm going roun' to aunt Marthy's to see 'bout it."

I bit my lips till the blood came to keep from crying out. Were my children with their grandmother, or had the speculator carried them off? The suspense was dreadful. Would Betty never come, and tell me the truth about it? At last she came, and I eagerly repeated what I had overheard. Her face was one broad, bright smile.

***

GO ON TO THE NEXT PAGE. ➡

Great surprise was expressed when it was known that my children had returned to their grandmother's. The news spread through the town, and many a kind word was bestowed on the little ones.

Dr. Flint went to my grandmother's to ascertain who was the owner of my children, and she informed him. "I expected as much," said he. "I am glad to hear it. I have had news from Linda lately, and I shall soon have her. You need never expect to see her free. She shall be my slave as long as I live, and when I am dead she shall be the slave of my children. If I ever find out that you or Phillip had any thing to do with her running off I'll kill him. And if I meet William in the street, and he presumes to look at me, I'll flog him within an inch of his life. Keep those brats out of my sight!"

As he turned to leave, my grandmother said something to remind him of his own doings. He looked back upon her, as if he would have been glad to strike her to the ground.

10   I had my season of joy and thanksgiving. It was the first time since my childhood that I had experienced any real happiness. I heard of the old doctor's threats, but they no longer had the same power to trouble me. The darkest cloud that hung over my life had rolled away. Whatever slavery might do to me, it could not shackle my children. If I fell a sacrifice, my little ones were saved. It was well for me that my simple heart believed all that had been promised for their welfare. It is always better to trust than to doubt.

¹**speculator:** a slave trader

11. What does <u>procured</u> mean in paragraph 2?

   A. built
   B. obtained
   C. saw
   D. needed

12. The reader learns that the narrator's children have been freed from slavery when the narrator

   A. overhears two women talking.
   B. knows Dr. Flint is in the house.
   C. asks Betty what has happened.
   D. sees them on the street.

13. In paragraph 10, the narrator says, "The darkest cloud that hung over my life had rolled away." This means that the narrator

   A. was relieved.
   B. felt angry.
   C. could see.
   D. was free.

14. The narrator is in danger because

   A. she is desperate to see her children.
   B. Betty has to open the trap door to bring her food.
   C. Dr. Flint is still searching for her.
   D. people outside can hear her talking.

15. Why did the narrator include the scene describing her vision of the children?

   A. To show how closely connected she felt to her children
   B. To provide an interesting diversion from her frightening story
   C. To prove that her children had escaped from slavery
   D. To illustrate how she calmed her fears through her dreams

16. After the narrator describes how her children were taken to be with her grandmother, why does she say that she had "no share in the rejoicings of that evening"?

   A. She was jealous because her children were free.
   B. She was hidden in another place.
   C. She was sad because her children were gone.
   D. She was on her way to the Free States.

GO ON TO THE NEXT PAGE. ➡

17. What contributes MOST to the suspense of the story?

    A. the darkness of the room the narrator is in

    B. the innocence of the narrator's children

    C. the separation of the narrator from her children

    D. what might happen if the narrator is caught

18. What does the narrator mean when she writes "my grandmother said something to remind him of his own doings"?

    A. The grandmother gives him news about his own family.

    B. The grandmother knows about crimes Dr. Flint has committed.

    C. The grandmother reminds him about something he needs to do.

    D. The grandmother accuses Dr. Flint of letting the narrator escape.

19. The author wrote this story to

    A. describe the life of slaves.

    B. inform readers about the evils of slavery.

    C. tell readers the story of one slave.

    D. persuade readers that slavery is evil.

20. The narrator's changing feelings throughout this excerpt can BEST be described as

    A. disbelief then belief.

    B. fear then relief.

    C. jealousy then forgiveness.

    D. confusion then understanding.

DIRECTIONS FOR QUESTION 21: Write your response in the space provided in the answer sheet section of this book.

21. In paragraph 10, the narrator says, "It was the first time since my childhood that I had experienced any real happiness."

    • What has happened to make her happy?

    • What might make her happy in the future?

Use information from the passage to support your answer.

END OF PART 3
Be sure to write your draft on the lined pages in the answer sheet section in the back of this book. You may check your work on this part only.

POSTTEST: PART 4
READING: NARRATIVE

In this part of the test, you will read a narrative passage and then respond to the multiple-choice and open-ended questions that follow it. You will have 30 minutes for this part of the test. You may look back at the passage and make notes in your test booklet if you like.

INTRODUCTION: *This excerpt is from the book* White Fang, *the story of an animal that is part dog, part wolf and his journey toward civilization. In this excerpt, two men and their sled dog team are being stalked by a pack of wolves.*

Excerpt from *White Fang*
by Jack London

They camped early that night. Three dogs could not drag the sled so fast nor for so long hours as could six, and they were showing unmistakable signs of playing out. And the men went early to bed, Bill first seeing to it that the dogs were tied out of gnawing-reach of one another.

But the wolves were growing bolder, and the men were aroused more than once from their sleep. So near did the wolves approach, that the dogs became frantic with terror, and it was necessary to replenish the fire from time to time in order to keep the adventurous marauders at safer distance.

"I've hearn sailors talk of sharks followin' a ship," Bill remarked, as he crawled back into the blankets after one such replenishing of the fire. "Well, them wolves is land sharks. They know their business better'n we do, an' they ain't a-holdin' our trail this way for their health. They're goin' to get us. They're sure goin' to get us, Henry."

"They've half got you a'ready, a-talkin' like that," Henry retorted sharply. "A man's half licked when he says he is. An' you're half eaten from the way you're goin' on about it."

"They've got away with better men than you an' me," Bill answered.

"Oh, shet up your croakin'. You make me all-fired tired."

Henry rolled over angrily on his side, but was surprised that Bill made no similar display of temper. This was not Bill's way, for he was easily angered by sharp words. Henry thought long over it before he went to sleep, and as his eyelids fluttered down and he dozed off, the thought in his mind was:

"There's no mistakin' it, Bill's almighty blue. I'll have to cheer him up to-morrow."

. . .

The day began <u>auspiciously</u>. They had lost no dogs during the night, and they swung out upon the trail and into the silence, the darkness, and the cold with spirits that were fairly light. Bill seemed to have forgotten his forebodings of the previous night, and even waxed facetious with the dogs when, at midday, they overturned the sled on a bad piece of trail. 8

It was an awkward mix-up. The sled was upside down and jammed between a tree-trunk and a huge rock, and they were forced to unharness the dogs in order to straighten out the tangle. The two men were bent over the sled and trying to right it, when Henry observed One Ear sidling away.

"Here, you, One Ear!" he cried, straightening up and turning around on the dog.

But One Ear broke into a run across the snow, his traces trailing behind him. And there, out in the snow of their back track, was the she-wolf waiting for him. As he neared her, he became suddenly cautious. He slowed down to an alert and mincing walk and then stopped. He regarded her carefully and dubiously, yet desirefully. She seemed to smile at him, showing her teeth in an ingratiating rather than a menacing way. She moved toward him a few steps, playfully, and then halted. One Ear drew near to her, still alert and cautious, his tail and ears in the air, his head held high.

He tried to sniff noses with her, but she retreated playfully and coyly. Every advance on his part was accompanied by

GO ON TO THE NEXT PAGE. ➡

a corresponding retreat on her part. Step by step she was luring him away from the security of his human companionship. Once, as though a warning had in vague ways flitted through his intelligence, he turned his head and looked back at the overturned sled, at his team-mates, and at the two men who were calling to him.

But whatever idea was forming in his mind, was dissipated by the she-wolf, who advanced upon him, sniffed noses with him for a fleeting instant, and then resumed her coy retreat before his renewed advances.

In the meantime, Bill had bethought himself of the rifle. But it was jammed beneath the overturned sled, and by the time Henry had helped him to right the load, One Ear and the she-wolf were too close together and the distance too great to risk a shot.

Too late One Ear learned his mistake. Before they saw the cause, the two men saw him turn and start to run back toward them. Then, approaching at right angles to the trail and cutting off his retreat they saw a dozen wolves, lean and grey, bounding across the snow. On the instant, the she-wolf's coyness and playfulness disappeared. With a snarl she sprang upon One Ear. He thrust her off with his shoulder, and, his retreat cut off and still intent on regaining the sled, he altered his course in an attempt to circle around to it. More wolves were appearing every moment and joining in the chase. The she-wolf was one leap behind One Ear and holding her own.

"Where are you goin'?" Henry suddenly demanded, laying his hand on his partner's arm.

Bill shook it off. "I won't stand it," he said. "They ain't a-goin' to get any more of our dogs if I can help it."

Gun in hand, he plunged into the underbrush that lined the side of the trail. His intention was apparent enough. Taking the sled as the centre of the circle that One Ear was making, Bill planned to tap that circle at a point in advance of the pursuit. With his rifle, in the broad daylight, it might be possible for him to awe the wolves and save the dog.

"Say, Bill!" Henry called after him. "Be careful! Don't take no chances!"

Henry sat down on the sled and watched. There was nothing else for him to do. Bill had already gone from sight; but now and again, appearing and disappearing amongst the underbrush and the scattered clumps of spruce, could be seen One Ear. Henry judged his case to be hopeless. The dog was thoroughly alive to its danger, but it was running on the outer circle while the wolf-pack was running on the inner and shorter circle. It was vain to think of One Ear so outdistancing his pursuers as to be able to cut across their circle in advance of them and to regain the sled.

The different lines were rapidly approaching a point. Somewhere out there in the snow, screened from his sight by trees and thickets, Henry knew that the wolf-pack, One Ear, and Bill were coming together. All too quickly, far more quickly than he had expected, it happened. He heard a shot, then two shots, in rapid succession, and he knew that Bill's ammunition was gone.

GO ON TO THE NEXT PAGE. ➡

22. Which of the following BEST describes Henry's feelings in the story?

    A. anxious, then hopeful
    B. curious, then frightened
    C. worried, then discouraged
    D. calm, then outraged

23. This story is MOSTLY about

    A. friends who are training for a dog sled race in the winter.
    B. two men and a team of dogs that encounter a pack of wolves.
    C. a trained sled dog that wants to escape into the wilderness.
    D. dog sled racers who accidentally overturn their sled.

24. Why did One Ear sneak away from Bill and Henry?

    A. He caught the scent of meat and followed it.
    B. He was tired and wanted to go to sleep.
    C. He started following another sled's trail and got lost.
    D. He was lured away by a female wolf.

25. Bill's and Henry's MAIN conflict in this story is that

    A. they have overturned their sled in the forest.
    B. their dogs are too tired to pull their sled fast.
    C. they are being stalked by a pack of hungry wolves.
    D. their dogs have pulled the sled off the main trail.

26. When the author says that Bill "seemed to have forgotten his forebodings of the previous night," he means that Bill

    A. isn't worried that they are moving slower than planned.
    B. doesn't care that some of the dogs have been killed.
    C. isn't concerned about the wolves anymore.
    D. doesn't remember what Henry said to him.

27. The mood of this story is

    A. suspenseful.
    B. peaceful.
    C. depressing.
    D. frustrating.

GO ON TO THE NEXT PAGE. ➡

28. What is the theme of the story?

   A. Friends should take care of one another.
   B. Things are not always as they seem.
   C. Fighting is not the way to solve problems.
   D. Man and nature are in constant struggle.

29. In paragraph 8, the word <u>auspiciously</u> means

   A. suspiciously.
   B. beautifully.
   C. frightfully.
   D. favorably.

30. Why does the author include Bill's story about sharks?

   A. to reduce the tension in the story
   B. to show how land and sea are alike
   C. to give hints about the final attack
   D. to reveal that Bill was once a sailor

31. What does the author mean by "the dog was thoroughly alive to its danger"?

   A. The dog was still alive and safe.
   B. The dog recognized the danger.
   C. The dog was completely afraid.
   D. The dog knew how to escape.

DIRECTIONS FOR QUESTION 32: Write your response in the space provided in the answer sheet section of this book.

32. Bill and Henry were alone in a frozen wilderness area with their sled dogs. They already had lost several dogs and were being stalked by ferocious wolves. If you were Bill

   • would you have gone off alone to rescue One Ear?

   • Why or why not?

   Use information from the story to support your answer.

DIRECTIONS FOR QUESTIONS 33 and 34: Write your response in the space provided in the answer sheet section of this book.

33. Why do you think Henry remained behind when Bill went after One Ear?

34. Would you have gone with Bill to find One Ear or would you bave stayed be-hind? Explain your answer.

POSTTEST: PART 4, Continued
WRITING: TO PERSUADE

This part of the test you will be asked to write a persuasive essay. Plan and draft your answer on a separate piece of paper. Revise and edit your draft. Then copy your final response into this book. If you finish ahead of time, do not go on to the next part of the test. Wait for your teacher to continue. You have 45 minutes to complete the writing task on the following page.

GO ON TO THE NEXT PAGE. ➡

WRITING SITUATION

Your parents arrived home from last night's city council meeting upset that the council is planning to cut down a century-old oak tree in the middle of the town square to make room for a new movie theater. The council members feel the tree's large branches are a danger to electrical lines and telephone poles, and they think the space could be utilized to build a movie theater that would bring more revenue into the city. Many city residents, however, think that the tree is a part of your town's heritage, and that cutting it down will only destroy what little history your town has left.

The council has decided to make its official decision on the removal of the tree after they hold a vote and get more feedback from the residents of the city. You decide to write the editor of your local newspaper about this decision.

WRITING TASK C

Write a letter to the local newspaper explaining your position on this issue. Use facts and examples to develop your argument.

Remember, if your letter gets published, you may have a chance to influence many readers.

LANGUAGE ARTS LITERACY

PREWRITING/PLANNING SPACE

When you finish your planning, copy your final response on the lined pages in the answer sheet section of this book.

END OF PART 4
Be sure to write your draft on the lined pages
in the answer sheet section at the back of this
book. You may check your work on this part only.

POSTTEST: PART 5
READING: INFORMATIONAL/EVERYDAY TEXT

In this part of the test, you will read an informational passage and then respond to the multiple-choice and open-ended questions that follow it. You will have 30 minutes to read the passage and answer the questions that follow. You may look back at the passage and make notes in your test booklet if you'd like.

Fin-tastic Savings!

When it comes to your underwater pets, you don't have to settle for anything less than the best. Starting January 15, Main Avenue Pet Supplies will be offering top name-brand aquarium equipment—everything you need to set up a great aquarium at discount prices. Here are just a few of the items in our inventory:

Starter Aquariums
2.5 gallon – $19.99
5 gallon – $29.99

Water Filter
Was $26.99,
now only $19.99!

Goldfish – $1.25 each

Floating Thermometer – $5.99

Aquarium Accessories – $4.99 to $10.99

Main Avenue Pet Supplies
7701 Main Avenue, Springfield
Open M–F 10-5, Saturday 12–4.

GO ON TO THE NEXT PAGE. ➡

The Ins and Outs of Aquariums

1 Have you ever had a flippered friend? Over the last century, fish have consistently been one of America's most preferred pets. Compared to most popular domestic animals, fish are low-maintenance creatures. They're well-behaved, too. They won't gnaw on furniture, shred curtains, or shed fur!

Setting up an aquarium can be an enjoyable project that calls on you not only to choose the conditions that would most benefit the fish, but also to make creative decisions that turn an aquarium into a piece of aquatic art. In order to construct an aquarium that's safe for fish and pleasing to the eye, follow these general guidelines. For more specific information, consult a specialist at your local pet shop.

You'll need a number of materials in order to get started. The most important item is, of course, the aquarium itself. Aquariums come in all shapes and sizes, from small one-gallon fishbowls meant for a single swimmer to giant tanks that can hold dozens of them.

4 After you've chosen the best aquarium, you'll need some special equipment to make it a safe and healthy <u>habitat</u> for your fish. You'll need aquarium gravel, a water filter, a water heater, a floating thermometer, and a pump.

Once you've acquired the necessary materials, the first step is to cleanse the aquarium of any grime, sediments, or other refuse that may have accumulated in it. Avoid using cleaning chemicals, though, since they can contaminate the water you later add to the aquarium. Once the aquarium is clean, add gravel to the bottom, typically one pound per gallon of water. You can even accessorize your aquarium with rocks, plants, or fanciful ornaments.

You'll want to install a filter in order to remove contaminants from the water and keep your fish healthy. Select a filter that's suitable for the size of your aquarium, and then install it according to the directions.

The next step is to fill the aquarium with clean, cool water; a safe guideline here is to only utilize water that you would consider drinkable. Don't fill the aquarium right to the top, though, because there are still a few subsequent items you'll need to add, including the water heater and pump. Install these appliances according to their directions. Usually, the heater should be adjusted to keep the water at a temperature of about seventy-five degrees Fahrenheit.

Then the fish will be more comfortable and healthy—unless you forget to add them! The most crucial component of an aquarium is, of course, the fish. Add them to the water and enjoy your new flippered friends.

GO ON TO THE NEXT PAGE. ➡

35. What does the word <u>habitat</u> mean in paragraph 4?

A. environment
B. location
C. temperature
D. lifespan

36. The advertisement was probably designed by a

A. store clerk.
B. fish expert.
C. salesperson.
D. pet lover.

37. The paragraph at the top of the ad suggests that Main Avenue Pet Supplies

A. has a wide variety of merchandise.
B. sells high-quality merchandise.
C. is well-known for its fish supplies.
D. sells many different kinds of fish.

38. The author begins the passage with a question to

A. show that fish are friendly.
B. get the reader's attention.
C. introduce an explanation.
D. provide background information.

39. Which word BEST describes the author's tone in the first paragraph?

A. serious
B. humorous
C. sentimental
D. objective

40. According to the advertisement, the most expensive item you will need to start an aquarium is the

A. tank.
B. filter.
C. fish.
D. thermometer.

41. In paragraph 1, what does the author mean by "fish are low-maintenance creatures"?

A. You must set up aquariums close to the floor.
B. Fish require expensive equipment to survive as indoor pets.
C. You can easily set up aquariums indoors using simple tools.
D. Fish are indoor pets that do not require a lot of special care.

GO ON TO THE NEXT PAGE. ➡

42. Why are pictures included with this passage?

A. to make it more attractive
B. to use the extra space
C. to show what each item looks like
D. to entertain and persuade readers

DIRECTIONS FOR QUESTION 50: Write your response in the space provided in the answer sheet section of this book.

43. The passage says fish are among America's most preferred pets.

• Would you like to have a fish as a pet?

• Why or why not?

END OF PART 5
Be sure to write your draft on the lined pages in the answer sheet section at the back of this book. You may check your work on this part only.

STOP

ASK8 Posttest Answer Key

Part 1 Writing Task A

Sample answer: When I heard that our class was going to the Aquarium, I wasn't really that thrilled. We went there in 4th grade and it was pretty boring. But when my teacher told me about the new exhibits I began looking forward to the trip. Before we went I went online and mapped out my route so that I could see my favorite parts first. My group would just have to follow my lead because I had a plan.

Luckily my group mates were pretty flexible and they didn't care what order we say each display. Since they are my ultimate favorite, we visited the sea turtles first. There were 15 turtles at the aquarium. The last time there weren't any turtles here. One of the workers was in the water with the turtles and she had one turtle swim by as I ran my hand over its bumpy shell. I think that I may want to be a marine biologist because I kept thinking how much I wanted her job! My group had to pry me away from the sea turtle exhibit.

As soon as I remembered our next stop, I forgot all about the turtles. Right around the corner was the shark tank. Now, I am absolutely terrified of sharks, but when they're behind twelve inches of reinforced glass, I get brave. The other members of my group seemed interested enough, but I just stood back and waited for it to appear. Sure enough, after a few minutes the darkest shadow in the farthest corner shifted and edged closer to the glass. This huge great white was at the aquarium the last time I visited and the last time I saw him I had nightmares for months. Soon it was me urging us to move to the next exhibit.

The dolphin show started at one o'clock which would give us just enough time to make it back to the bus when it was over. This was the perfect way to end the day because those dolphins have so much energy that they make you smile. If I was an animal, I wonder if I would get so much enjoyment entertaining people. The dolphins put us all in a good mood with their amazing stunts and tricks.

As we left the aquarium, we had just enough time to visit the souvenir shop. Everything was really expensive, but I bought a turtle magnet, a shark pen, and a dolphin bookmark to remember that great trip. The next time I'm not looking forward to going somewhere, I will remember this trip and how much fun I had with my group.

Explanation:

The response fulfills all aspects of the prompt and appropriately addresses the audience. The writing is focused, follows a single format, and is well organized. There are very few, if any, mistakes in grammar, mechanics, punctuation, and capitalization. The supportive details and examples are interesting, appropriate and relevant.

Part 2 Informational

1. **C.** Interpreting literary elements (G16)

   The author is using imagery to capture the idea of dragons as creatures of myth that are beyond the experience of our everyday world. Therefore, answer choice C is the correct answer.

2. **B.** Recognizing supporting details (G20)

    The passage says that the body parts of dragons in ancient China usually resembled those of other animals. Answer choice B is correct.

3. **C.** Drawing conclusions (G20, G21)

    The author has found many interesting details about the history of dragons around the world. He is obviously very interested in, or fascinated by, them. Answer choice C is correct.

4. **D.** Recognizing purpose (G10, G20)

    The passage is informational, and it gives readers information about dragons in ancient China.

5. **A.** Recognizing supporting details (G20)

    This answer is stated in the passage. When people in ancient Japan were not allowed to see their emperors, they believed it was because their emperors had turned into dragons. Answer choice A is the correct answer.

6. **A.** Interpreting words (F1)

    When people conversed with dragons, they talked to them. Answer choice A is the correct answer.

7. **C.** Recognizing a central idea (E1)

    The central idea of the article is that dragons have held an important place in and exerted many influences on Chinese society from ancient times until today. Choice C is the correct answer.

8. **C.** Extrapolating meaning (G21)

    The author seems interested in dragons because they mean different things to different people. Therefore, answer choice C is the correct answer.

9. **C.** Interpreting words (F1)

The word *narratives* is a plural noun that means stories or accounts of events. A narrator is a person who tells stories. Answer choice C is the correct answer.

10. Drawing conclusions (G20, G21)

Sample answer: *In ancient China, people believed that dragons affected almost all aspects of their lives. For example, peasants and emperors in ancient China believed that dragons protected their lands and helped their families. They also believed that if a dragon was displeased with them, it might cause floods or droughts to punish them.*

Part 3 Narrative

11. **B.** Paraphrasing/retelling (F1)

The sentence in paragraph 2 that uses the word "procured" says, "My uncle procured a wagon and carried William and the children back to town." This sentence describes how the author's uncle used a wagon to take the people to town. He did not have time to build a wagon, and he did not just need a wagon or see a wagon. Therefore, the correct answer is B: obtained.

12. **C.** Recognition of supporting details (G20)

The narrator has a vision or a dream about her children. Then she hears two women talking about them, but she is still not sure what happened, so she asks Betty. Answer choice C is the correct answer.

13. **A.** Predicting meaning (G8, G20)

This question asks you to interpret a figurative term. The narrator says she feels like a dark cloud had just rolled out of her life. Considering that she said this after learning her children were free from slavery, we can understand that she was relieved. Answer choice A is correct.

14. **C.** Drawing conclusions (G20, G21)

The narrator has many dangers in her life, but once she is hidden away, she is safer. At that time, the greatest danger she faces is that Dr. Flint is still searching for her. He questions people, including her own family, on her whereabouts, and vows to recapture her. Answer choice C is the correct answer.

15. **A.** Recognizing organizational structure (G12)

Earlier in the same paragraph where the narrator describes her vision or dream, she says she was thinking of her children when the sound of a song outside reminded her of the moaning of children. In this moment of sadness, her children seem to appear before her. The best answer is choice A.

16. **B.** Extrapolation of information (G21)

All through the excerpt, the narrator explains how she would willingly sacrifice herself to see her children safe. So she is not jealous. She may be unhappy to be apart from them, but that is not the reason for her comment. She has not escaped; she is in hiding to protect her from Dr. Flint. Therefore, B is the best answer.

17. **D.** Interpreting textual conventions and literary elements (G8)

There are several reasons that a story like this is suspenseful. However, the best reason is that the reader doesn't know what will happen to the narrator if she's captured. Therefore, answer choice D is the best answer.

18. **B.** Predicting meaning (G8, G20)

The narrator has just described all the threats made by Dr. Flint against her family. As the scene ends, the doctor looked "as if he would have been glad to strike her." Therefore, the grandmother would likely have said something to show that she knew about his other cruelties. Answer B is the best choice.

19. **C.** Recognizing author's purpose (G10, G20)

Although the end result could be that readers realize that slavery is evil, the author's purpose is to share the story of one woman and her suffering as a slave. Choice C is the best answer.

20. **B.** Drawing conclusions (G20, G21)

Throughout the passage, the narrator describes her terror as she waited for word about her children. She then expresses relief that Dr. Flint's threats no longer had the same power over her once she knew her children were safe.

21. Drawing conclusions (G20, G21)

Sample answer:

The narrator has learned that her children are now free from slavery and Dr. Flint, and this has made her very happy. She says that whatever slavery might do to her, it can no longer touch her children. She would be extremely happy in the future if she were allowed to be reunited with her children.

Part 4 Narrative

22. **C.** Drawing conclusions (G20, G21)

In the beginning of the story, both Bill and Henry seem worried about the wolves following their sled. Later, Henry watches Bill run after the wolves and feels hopeless about their situation. Answer choice C is the best answer.

23. **B.** Recognizing a central idea (E)

The story never mentions that Bill and Henry are in a race, which eliminates choices A and D. Although One Ear does get distracted by the she-wolf, he's not looking to escape into the wild. The correct answer is B.

24. **D.** Recognizing supporting details (G20)

One Ear got distracted by the she-wolf. She was acting playful and led him away from the safety of his owners. Answer choice D is correct.

25. **C.** Interpreting literary elements (G)

Answer choice D is not a conflict in the story. Choices, A, B, and C are all conflicts in the story. However, the main conflict is choice C: Bill and Henry are being followed by a pack of wolves that keeps attacking their dogs.

26. **C.** Predicting meaning (G8, G20)

In this sentence, the word "forebodings" means concerns that something bad might happen. The previous night, Bill was worried that he and Henry would lose another dog to the wolves. However, when he wakes up, he seems happier and less worried. The correct answer is C.

27. **A.** Interpreting literary elements (G16)

The mood of this story is certainly not peaceful. Bill and Henry are being followed by a pack of wolves that keeps attacking their dogs. While it may seem depressing or frustrating in some parts, the cliffhanger ending makes the mood in the story suspenseful. Answer choice A is correct.

28. **D.** Recognizing a theme (E1)

This story illustrates the struggle between man and nature. Man is represented by Bill and Henry. Nature is represented by the wolves in the wilderness.

29. **D.** Retelling/paraphrasing (F1)

To determine the meaning, read the sentences that follow. The men have light spirits, Bill seems happier, and they lost no dogs to the wolves. There's nothing suspicious or frightening in the scene and no descriptions of the surrounding area that could be considered beautiful. The day has begun on a favorable note. Answer choice D is the best answer.

30. **C.** Recognizing organizational structure (G)

Bill's story about the sharks gives an ominous tone to the story. It increases rather than reduces the tension. The correct answer choice is C.

31. **B.** Predicting meaning (G8, G20)

To determine the meaning, read the entire phrase. It says nothing about fear or escape. The dog is alive, as in choice A, but that choice does not cover the meaning of the entire phrase. The only choice that reflects the full meaning is choice B: the dog recognized the danger.

32.   Forming of opinions (G20, G21)

Sample answer.

If I were Bill, I would not have gone after One Ear. Bill himself told Henry about sharks and how they hunted sailors on the high seas. Bill saw for himself that the wolves were using similar tactics as they followed the men on the trail. I think Bill was rash to leave Henry alone. I understand that he wanted to save a valuable sled dog, but I think I would have worked with my friend. I think that would give both of us a better chance to survive a dangerous situation.

33.   Extrapolating information (G21)

Sample answer.

I think Henry is more practical than Bill. Henry seems like a person who tries to deal with life as best he can by planning when he can, but not worrying about things he can't control. For example, he rejects Bill's worries about wolves acting like land sharks. He believes that getting so upset about what could happen just puts them in more danger. At the end, when Bill goes after the pack and One Ear, Henry just tells him to be careful. He seems to understand that he can't change Bill's mind. Then, as he watches, he tries to analyze what Bill, One Ear, and the pack are doing so he can understand what the outcome may be. When he hears Bill's final shot, he knows his friend and One Ear are doomed.

34.   Forming of opinions (G20, G21)

Sample answer.

It is tough to predict what I might do in such a desperate situation. Before venturing out into the wilderness on such an adventure, I would have planned for this type of situation the way Bill and Henry had. I would make use of the sled, the gun, and all our resources.

I wouldn't want to stay behind because then we would both be in more danger since we would each be alone. I would think wolves would have an easier time ganging up on you if you were alone. Additionally, I would feel helpless and useless sitting there waiting for Bill to save One Ear. If I went with Bill, we would be together but may run the risk of getting lost or attacked. Our best bet may be to leave One Ear, but I don't think I could do that either. Our best chance of fighting off the wolves and saving One Ear would be to work together. The wolves have the advantage in numbers, so we would need to make up for their advantage somehow.

Like Bill, I would have a hard time letting the wolves win. It would bother me even more that the wolves would attack a fellow canine. Pausing to think about the best way to enter a situation could mean the difference between you living or dying. Working together and staying together would be my preference in this situation.

Explanation: *This response is not meant to be as long as that of essay answers. The answer clearly responds to the questions and explains using details and examples. There is a clear opening and closing. The writer stays focused on the topic, addresses the audience appropriately, and flows nicely from beginning to end.*

Part 4 Writing To Persuade

Sample answer:

To the City Council:

I have just learned of your plans to cut down the oak tree in the center of town square. The thought of losing another historical landmark of our town saddens me. The old oak tree has been a part of so many lives. When my great-grandparents got married, they were photographed under the old oak. We have pictures of my grandmother and grandfather as toddlers swinging from the branches. They too were photographed there on their wedding day, as were my parents. On my bedroom wall, I have a photograph of my best friend and me attempting to  *climb the massive tree when we were barely old enough to walk. Obviously, this tree has been around for many generations, and I always hoped that one day my own children would get to experience the joy of sitting under the old oak on a hot, summer day.*

I understand that one reason given for the removal of the tree is that the branches might impede the poles and wires. It's never been a problem for city workers to trim these branches before. Why is it a problem now? I think the bigger issue is that you want to build a movie theater to bring in more money. The last thing this town needs is another movie theater. We already have a cinema at each end of town. Is it really necessary to add another? These massive buildings, with their long lines and gaudy lights, detract from the natural beauty of our town. Why destroy the one glorious work of nature we have left? I urge you to think very carefully before you plow under another historical landmark.

Part 5 Informational/Everyday Text

35. **A.** Paraphrasing/retelling (F1)

The article says that you can create a safe and healthy habitat for your fish. The words "safe and healthy" imply more than just a location. The passage does not discuss details such as temperature or the lifespan of a fish. Answer choice A, environment, is the best answer choice.

36. **C.** Recognizing purpose (G10, G20)

This question asks you to determine who designed the advertisement. This requires you to consider the reason why or purpose for the advertisement. Because the advertisement is trying to sell supplies, "salesperson" is the best answer choice.

37. **B.** Drawing conclusions (G20, G21)

The paragraph says, " . . . you don't have to settle for anything less than the best" and that they carry "top brand names." Therefore, answer choice B is the best answer.

38. **B.** Recognizing organizational structure (G)

The author begins the passage with a question to get readers' attention. Answer choice B is the correct answer. The other answer choices do not really apply to this passage.

39. **B.** Interpreting textual conventions and literary elements (G16)

The author has a humorous tone. He refers to fish as "flippered friends" and says they will not gnaw furniture, shred curtains, or shed fur.

40. **A.** Recognizing supporting details/Interpreting segments of text (G)

To answer this question, you have to look at the ad. Because a fish tank starts at $19.99, it is the most expensive item.

41. **D.** Predicting meaning (G8, G20)

To answer this and similar types of questions asking you to predict meaning, do not get distracted by unimportant details. Look at the entire phrase and the sentences that follow. The author is clearly indicating that fish are easy pets to own. Therefore, answer choice D is the correct answer: Fish do not require a lot of special care.

42. **C.** Recognizing organizational structure (G)

Pictures do enhance the appearance of the article. However, the article's primary purpose is to interest people in aquariums who may not be familiar with them. Therefore, the pictures are there to show readers what each item looks like. Answer choice C is the best answer.

43. Forming opinions (G20, G21)

Sample Answer:

I would not want to own a fish. Some people may consider fish works of art, but to me, the various sizes, shapes, and colors of cats and dogs are much more beautiful than any fish inside an aquarium. Although I can see why some people like the idea that a fish does not chew furniture or shed fur, fish also cannot come out of the tank to play with you. The most important reason I would own a pet is for companionship. I want to have an animal that can cuddle on my lap or sit by my side, play with me, and maybe even go outside with me.

Appendix

This appendix provides you with opportunities to review and practice other aspects of the Language Arts Literacy program in New Jersey. These Language Arts areas include Speaking, Listening, and Viewing.

Speaking (Standard 3.3)

Good speeches require good speaking skills, but they also require good planning skills. Suppose you are given a task to explain a topic to an audience. To explain your ideas effectively, you will first need to organize them in a way that makes sense to you.

For an assignment, you will most often be provided with a topic, or theme. Once you know what the theme of your speech will be, you should follow certain steps to create a good composition that you can present with confidence.

 ## Lesson 1: Planning Your Speech

This lesson covers the following standard for speaking (D7, D8, D15, D17). Writing a speech that:

- responds clearly and appropriately to the given prompt.
- selects a focus and appropriate details to support it.
- use clear and concise language.
- is organized and includes an introduction, conclusion, and transitions.
- uses elaboration to engage the audience.

- uses conventions of spoken English and specific conventions of speech.

- is conscious of and uses varied sentence structure and word choice.

- expresses interest in a topic.

- makes generalizations and leads audience toward a conclusion.

Giving a speech in front of a live audience can sometimes be a little frightening. However, you can help to curb some of your fear by making sure that you are well prepared to deliver your speech. Writing a speech is a lot like writing an essay. You have to pay attention to the content and organization of your speech, your word usage, your sentence construction, and your mechanics. You should begin writing your speech using the three stages of writing. As you learned in Part 2 of this book, the three stages of writing are **prewriting**, **drafting**, and **revising**.

Prewriting— RECORD Your Ideas

Once you know what theme you will be explaining in your speech, write down some ideas about that topic on a piece of paper. Try to look at the topic from different angles. At this point, neatness is not important—as long as you can read what you wrote!

Suppose your task is to write a speech about lowering the voting age from 18 to 16:

Theme: Lowering the Voting Age

Many people have debated whether or not to change the voting age from eighteen to sixteen. Some think that sixteen-year-olds are too young to vote on important decisions, such as who will run the country as the next president. Others feel that allowing youthful opinions to affect our government would improve the way in which the country is run.

Task: Write and deliver a speech explaining why you think it is or is not a good idea to lower the voting age to sixteen.

How will you come up with a speech on this theme? A good way to start is to write down some ideas about the theme. What if you haven't decided how you feel about the theme? Recording your ideas is a good way to sort out your opinions. For example, you could list the positive and negative aspects, or pros and cons, of your issue to help you decide which stand you will take in your speech:

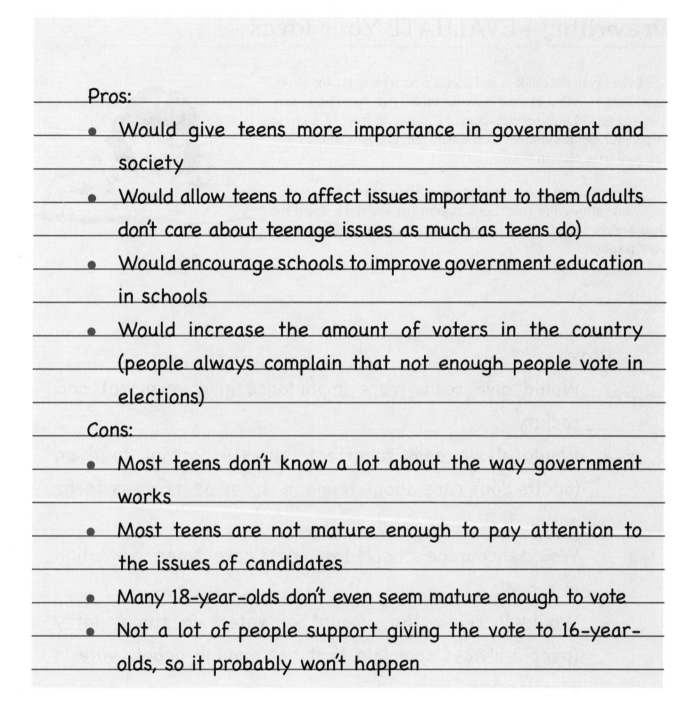

Pros:

- Would give teens more importance in government and society
- Would allow teens to affect issues important to them (adults don't care about teenage issues as much as teens do)
- Would encourage schools to improve government education in schools
- Would increase the amount of voters in the country (people always complain that not enough people vote in elections)

Cons:

- Most teens don't know a lot about the way government works
- Most teens are not mature enough to pay attention to the issues of candidates
- Many 18-year-olds don't even seem mature enough to vote
- Not a lot of people support giving the vote to 16-year-olds, so it probably won't happen

Which ideas are most convincing to you? Choose the side that you feel is stronger. Now you are ready to evaluate your ideas.

Prewriting—EVALUATE Your Ideas

Look over your list of ideas and decide which ideas are the strongest. This is called evaluating your ideas. Are there any ideas that you would not feel confident explaining in front of a group of people? Get rid of them. You should feel good about the ideas that you have chosen to keep.

Suppose you have decided to explain why 16-year-olds *should* be allowed to vote. Look at your list and think about the theme of the speech. Then get rid of ideas that won't help support your position.

Pros:

- Would give teens more importance in government and society

- Would allow teens to affect issues important to them (adults don't care about teenage issues as much as teens do)

- ~~Would encourage schools to improve government education in schools~~

- Would increase the amount of voters in the country (people always complain that not enough people vote in elections)

Your speech is really about allowing 16-year-olds to vote, not about improving the country's educational system, so you may choose to eliminate this idea. Now it is time to organize the ideas you have chosen to explain in your speech.

Prewriting—ORGANIZE Your Ideas

A good speech is organized into three parts:

1. **Introduction**—In the speech's introduction, you will present your topic and explain why the topic should be discussed. Ask yourself why the topic is an important one. Your answers will help you form your introduction.

2. **Main ideas**—The main ideas are the ones you have chosen to explain in your speech. In this section of the speech, your main ideas should be clearly explained. State your opinions, and then support them with examples.

3. **Conclusion**—In the conclusion of your speech, you should present a short summary of your ideas. Briefly restate your ideas and explain why they are good, or what good things will happen if your ideas are carried out.

Drafting—Begin Your FIRST DRAFT

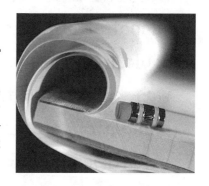

Now it is time to start the writing process. Begin explaining your ideas, paying attention to the organization suggested in Step 3. It is not necessary to record your ideas perfectly the first time you write them down— this is why it is called a first draft! You will revise and edit your draft in the next step.

Your first draft may look something like this:

> Some people think that teenagers aren't mature and make bad decisions. But this perception may be because of the fact that teenagers aren't given enough important responsibilties. 16-year-olds have the important responsibilities that they can drive. They can also hold part-time jobs, and many excel at it. But what if 16-years-olds were given the most important responsibility of all, which is the right to vote?
>
> Teenagers have a lot of important opinions, but often aren't taken seriously. People who think that teen agers only care

about socializing with their friends may not be listening to them. If teenagers were given the right to vote, citizens would be forced to listen to the younger population. If teenagers could vote, both society and the government might realize that the teenage population is a valuable part of America. Once voting teens had a valid and noticeable voice, they would be able to effect issues important to the younger population. Perhaps if teenagers who felt not safe in schools had the power to affect gun control laws, the country might see less occurrences of weapons and violence in schools. If teenagers whose parents cannot afford nightly meals were allowed to vote, perhaps they could help convince the government to make sure that no child was hungry. Lastly if teenagers had the right to vote, the number of voters in the country would increase, because people often complain about the lack of voters in elections, and the lack of interest in candidates in general. Teenagers are typically passionate and this country needs more passionate voters to show the importance of exercsing the right to vote.

It is my opinion that giving 16-year-olds the right to vote would improve the country in many ways because older American citizens would learn to listen to teenagers if their opinions were equal to those of adults counted as much as the opinions of adults do, and if lawmakers respected and incorporated teenager's ideas into our government, we could solve many issues that currently plage us by focusing on what is important to our youthful. Any right given to a group of people who did not have that right is a precious gift. And if teenagers were given the right to vote, I suspect that most would be careful and responsible to prove that they deserve to be heard. And if adults witnessed teenagers exercising their voting responsibilities seriously, maybe more adults would pay attention to the issues and get out to the polls to improve the state of our country. We are all citizens regardless of age and our voices shall all be heard.

Revising and Editing—Writing the FINAL DRAFT

Review the skills for revising and editing found in Part 2 of this book. Once you have revised your first draft for clarity and spelling, perhaps your final speech will look something like this:

Many people think that teenagers are immature and make bad decisions, but this perception may be a result of the fact that teenagers aren't given enough important responsibilities. Sixteen-year-olds are given the important responsibilities of driving and holding part-time jobs, and many excel in these areas. But what if sixteen-year-olds were given the most important responsibility of all—the right to vote?

Teenagers have many important opinions, but often aren't taken seriously. People who think that teenagers only care about socializing with friends may not be listening. If teenagers had the right to vote, American citizens would be forced to listen to the ideas and opinions of the younger population, and would likely find something of value in the voices of their children and grandchildren. Once voting teens had a valid and noticeable voice, they would be able to affect issues important to the younger population. Perhaps if teenagers who felt unsafe in schools had the power to affect gun control laws, the country might see fewer occurrences of weapons and violence in schools. If teenagers whose parents cannot afford nightly meals were allowed to vote, perhaps they could help to make sure that no child was hungry. Lastly, people often complain about the lack of voters in elections, and the lack of interest in candidates in general, but if teenagers had the right to vote, the number of voters in the country would increase. Teenagers are typically passionate, and this country needs more passionate voters to demonstrate the importance of exercising the right to vote.

It is my opinion that giving sixteen-year-olds the right to vote would improve the country in many ways. Older American citizens would learn to listen to teenagers if their opinions were equal to those of adults, and if lawmakers respected and incorporated teenagers' ideas into our government, we could solve many issues that currently plague us by focusing on what is important to our youthful citizens. Any right given to a group of people who did not previously have that right is a precious gift, and if teenagers were given the right to vote, I suspect that most would be careful and responsible to prove that they deserve to be heard. And if adults witnessed teenagers exercising their voting responsibilities seriously, maybe more adults would pay attention to the issues and get out to the polls to improve the state of our country. We are all citizens, regardless of age, and our voices should all be heard.

Lesson 2: Speaking Skills

This lesson covers the following skills for speaking (A1, A4, A6, A8, B1, B2, B3, B6, C3, D1, D3). Delivering a speech that:

- responds clearly and appropriately to a given prompt.

- selects a focus and appropriate details to support it.

- is organized and includes an introduction, conclusion, and transitions.

- uses elaboration to engage the audience.

- uses conventions of spoken English and specific conventions of speech.

- is conscious of and uses varied sentence structure and word choice.

- expresses an interest in the topic.

- allows interaction with the audience and adjustments to sustain engagement.

- makes generalizations and leads the audience toward a conclusion.

Now that your writing is complete, you should start thinking about how you are going to present your speech.

Speaking—SHOW and TELL Your Ideas

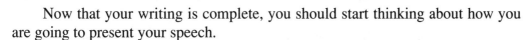

Visual aids will help you show the audience what you are saying, and note cards will help you remember what to tell your audience. Many people find it helpful, however, to create their note cards before they start to think about their visual aids.

Note cards will help keep you on track while you are delivering your speech. When creating a set of note cards for a speech, you should remember a few important things.

Notes about Note Cards

- **Do not read your speech straight from your cards.** Note cards are there to guide you, but you should not rely on them for the entire content of your speech.

- **Your cards should contain key phrases.** These phrases will help guide you through your speech. Once you have practiced your speech a few times, you will have a good idea of what you are going to say next. However, you may forget which point comes next in your speech, and this is where note cards will help you. It is a good idea to have a few different cards for each part of your speech.

- **Write key phrases in large print.** You want to see what is written on your cards without looking at them too much, or without holding them in directly front of your face.

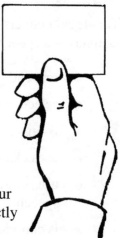

Visualizing Your Visual Aids

Visual aids can entertain your audience by giving them something to look at, but they should not distract the audience. Their purpose is to support and strengthen the points that you are explaining. In fact, in some cases, they may closely resemble your note cards.

Speakers often use many different types of visual aids to strengthen the points in their speeches, including charts, graphs, video, slides, computer presentations, and others. Whether or not you use visual aids to support your speech for this test is up to you. Because you have a limited amount of time to prepare your speech, you will want to stick to simple visual aids. Often a bulleted list of points is an effective visual aid.

Overall, visual aids should be colorful, but not distracting, and clear enough that a person in the back of the audience can see them.

Speaking—PRACTICE Makes Perfect

Once the writing stage is finished and you have made your note cards and visual aids, you should practice reciting your speech aloud a few times before you deliver it to your audience, time permitting. You can also practice your speech in front of a mirror, if one is available, to see how you will be viewed by others while delivering your speech.

Keep the following tips in mind while practicing your speech:

- Speak in a loud voice, but do not shout.

- Speak slowly and pronounce your words clearly.

- Pay attention to time—you may need to speed up or slow down a bit to fit your speech to the amount of time that you are given.

- Maintain good eye contact with your audience.

- Use gestures to engage your audience.

- Do not read your speech directly off your note cards.

- Keep your note cards down, away from your face.

- Decide which points should be emphasized by changing the tone of your voice (called *intonation*)—you should stress important points to get your audience's attention.

- Be prepared to answer any questions that your audience may have.

SPEAKING

Prepare the following:

Theme: Length of the School Year

Many people have considered changing the way that American students are educated, without changing the amount of days that students attend school. Some think that students might get a better education if the school year was 12 months long, with more frequent breaks. Others think that the current system, in which students attend school for 9½ months and then have a 2½-month-long summer vacation, works very well.

TASK: Write and deliver a speech in which you explain why you do or do not think that the school year should be extended to 12 months.

Sample Speech:

When discussing the possibility of changing the length of the school year, several issues become important factors. The first consideration is whether one long disruption in students' education or several short ones will best benefit students. Second, we should think about the same issue in relation to teachers, and lastly, we need to consider how students would feel about giving up the long stretch of summer vacation that we have all become used to.

Students seem to perform best when working hard in spurts, but are our current spurts too long? While most students have fresh minds at the start of the school year in September, many are struggling and overworked by the time winter break arrives. The stretch of continuous schooling after this break is even longer, and many students are burned-out by the time summer vacation rolls around. Though students currently get a few days off here and there during the school year, if students were provided with longer, more frequent breaks, they might not experience this fatigue and may feel more mentally alert and able to retain what they are learning. It is easy to imagine that teachers feel the same fatigue, and would benefit from the 12-month school year in the same ways that students would. As long as the breaks were long enough, say, three weeks, most students probably wouldn't mind giving up their summer vacations because they would have several mini-vacations throughout the year.

I think that the 12-month school year would greatly benefit students. Frequent breaks would take off some of the pressure that students often feel when approaching one of the few breaks that they currently have. Such breaks would also allow both students and teachers to maintain a constant level of mental clarity, rather than pushing their brains to the limit and then collapsing, as is currently very common. Most students would probably agree that frequent, small vacations are better than one long one, as well. If the 12-month school year is executed, generations of students to come may achieve higher grades and higher levels of college acceptance, which is ultimately why the 12-month school year is such a good idea.

GRADING

The New Jersey State Department of Education grades speaking tasks on a 4-point scale.

Elements of a 4-Point Speech
Content/Organization:

- Maintains a clear focus on a central idea or topic
- Elaborates details to support central idea
- Has an opening or closing
- Includes a clearly stated conclusion/opinion that is linked to central idea or topic
- Uses varied sentence structure and word choice

Delivery (Spoken):

- Clearly attends to the audience through good eye contact and gestures
- Speaks audibly with expression; uses pacing and intonation effectively

Lesson 3: Listening
(Standard 3.4)

Active listening is an intricate part of your Language Arts Literacy program. During this year you will have the opportunity to develop an awareness of the intonation, rhythm, pace, volume and quality of what you hear. Active listening will greatly increase you ability to respond to others appropriately.

This exercise will help you to review the following skills: (A1, A2, A3, A4, A5, B2, B5, B6, B7).

Ask someone who is an articulate reader to read the following story to you. Do not look at the story—and do not take notes. Allow your listening skills to carry the responsibility for the information that you will need to answer the questions that follow.

Give yourself 25 minutes to listen to the passage and answer questions 1 through 8. Listen carefully because you cannot take notes.

Learning to accept criticism can be difficult. Here is a story about a boy who asks his grandfather to critique his writing.

Ouch!

1 Enrico slipped off his jacket and tossed it on the lawn beside him. The bright sun had warmed the chilly morning air. Enrico picked up a marigold and began removing the dirt around its roots before placing it into one of the shallow holes he and his grandfather had dug. "No, no, Enrico, don't do that," his grandfather gently chided. "It's better to leave the root ball intact. If you break off the soil, you might damage the roots and kill the plant."

Enrico smiled and placed the flower in the hole with the roots and surrounding soil intact. His grandfather, his *abuelo*, was a man of great experience and wisdom. He had taught Enrico many things throughout the years. He had taught him the importance of using good-quality lumber when they built a garden shed together in the backyard. Under his grandfather's guidance, Enrico had learned how to make the world's greatest tortillas using peppers so hot they burned your lips. Most of the novels Enrico devoured at night were his grandfather's picks. Grandfather often recommended a new read for Enrico, usually one that was obscure but wonderful, the kind of book you might find at a yard sale rather than on a bestsellers list.

Now Enrico wanted his grandfather to teach him how to be a better writer. Even though he had learned English as a second language, Grandfather had become adept enough to publish several history books and had worked for many years as a news reporter for their local paper. "I want to be a writer," Enrico announced as he gently pushed the soil around the marigold so it stood straight in its new home. "I've actually

written several short stories. I was hoping you would read them and tell me what you think—and not just tell me that they're good. I want your guidance, so I can improve my writing abilities and become a published writer."

Grandfather shook his head. "Ah, I don't know, Enrico. It isn't easy having your writing critiqued, and I wouldn't want to chance hurting your feelings. You're a bright young man. If you choose to become a writer, you will be a good one, with or without my help."

Despite his grandfather's warnings, however, Enrico finally persuaded him to critique one of his short stories. Enrico selected his best piece: a tale about a boy who was the smallest and worst player on his basketball team. The boy, Miguel, was often teased by the other players for his lack of height and skill. Enrico had revised the story several times until he was certain that his command of the English language was at its best. He printed a copy of the story and left it on his grandfather's kitchen table with a note on top that said, "Tell the truth, Grandfather. I can take it, really I can. And I greatly appreciate your help."

After school the next day Enrico rushed to his grandfather's house. "Did you read it?"

GO ON TO THE NEXT PAGE. ➡

he asked, as his grandfather rubbed a wet dish with a towel and placed it on a shelf.

"Of course I read it, son," Grandfather said and grinned, "and I think you're a very good writer."

Feeling frustrated, Enrico sighed and plopped in a kitchen chair. This was not what he wanted to hear. "Could you give me more than that?" he asked as he ran his fingers through his hair. "Could you tell me what is good about the story and what is bad? Please?"

Grandfather pulled out a chair and sat down beside Enrico. He picked up the printout of Enrico's story. "You need to show more and tell less, for starters," Grandfather advised. "For example, don't tell the reader that Miguel had a sad look on his face. What about Miguel's face looked sad? Describe his face and let your readers draw their own conclusion." Enrico nodded. "And your plot is so predictable that I knew Miguel was going to score the winning basket after reading only the first paragraph. Why not have him miss the shot, but impress his teammates with his newly acquired skill?"

Enrico frowned. "Ouch!" he exclaimed. "Wasn't there *anything* you liked about my story?"

Grandfather laughed loudly. "I told you it's tough to hear criticism regarding your writing. Writing is a process and, as a writer, your work must undergo many revisions. This is normal, Enrico."

"Maybe I don't have the talent to become a published writer," Enrico confessed, doubting himself.

"You definitely have the talent, but do you have the perseverance? Great writers do not give up. They keep on revising until they get it right."

Enrico smiled. "I hear what you're saying and I won't give up. I'm ready to try again, and I will keep trying until my work is as good as it can be," Enrico said. Grandfather shook his hand. "That's my boy," he said. "I am very proud of you."

GO ON TO THE NEXT PAGE. ➡

1. Why doesn't Grandfather want to read Enrico's story?

   A. He does not think it will be any good.
   B. He does not enjoy suggesting changes.
   C. He does not want to hurt Enrico's feelings.
   D. He does not believe Enrico will listen to him.

2. Read this sentence from from paragraph 1.

   "No, no, Enrico, don't do that," his grandfather gently chided.

   What does the word *chided* mean?

   A. claimed
   B. corrected
   C. concealed
   D. challenged

3. What is one problem with the story Enrico has written?

   A. The outcome is obvious.
   B. The first paragraph is too long.
   C. The main character is ordinary.
   D. The language needs improvement.

4. The title of the story, "Ouch!" captures

   A. how Grandfather feels.
   B. how Enrico feels.
   C. the title of Enrico's story.
   D. how Miguel feels.

5. How does Enrico feel about his Grandfather?

   A. sympathetic
   B. annoyed
   C. suspicious
   D. appreciative

6. Which technique does the author use to establish the theme of this passage?

   A. repetition
   B. personification
   C. dialogue
   D. flashback

GO ON TO THE NEXT PAGE. ➡

DIRECTIONS FOR QUESTION 7: Write your response in the space provided in the answer sheet section of this book.

7. The story says that Enrico wants to become a writer.

   • Based on what you heard, list two adjectives that describe Enrico.

   • Explain how these character traits might help him become a writer.

   Use details and information from the story to support your answer.

DIRECTIONS FOR QUESTION 8: Write your response in the space provided in the answer sheet section of this book.

8. In the beginning of the story the author says that Grandfather learned English as a second language and that he "had become adept enough to publish several history books and had worked for many years as a news reporter for their local paper."

   • Tell why the author included this detail.

   • Explain how this detail relates to the central idea of the story.

   Use information and details from the story to support your answer.

Listening Answer Key

1. **C.**   Recognition of supporting details (A2)

   Grandfather says that he does not think it's a good idea for him to review Enrico's story because it's sometimes difficult to accept criticism and he would not want to hurt Enrico's feelings.

2. **B.**   Paraphrasing/retelling (B5)

   When Grandfather says "No, no, Enrico, don't do that," he is correcting Enrico. "Correcting" and "chiding" have nearly the same meaning.

3. **A.**   Recognition of supporting details (A2)

   Grandfather says that he predicted the outcome of Enrico's story after reading the first paragraph. Therefore, answer choice A is the correct answer.

4. **B.**   Interpretation of conventions of speech (B1)

   Enrico says "ouch!" when Grandfather criticizes his short story. The title "Ouch!" describes how Enrico feels when Grandfather tells him what is wrong with his story.

5. **D.** Drawing conclusions (B2)

   Enrico is appreciative of the many different ways his grandfather helps him. You can also eliminate incorrect answer choices to find the correct answer to this question.

6. **C.**   Interpretation of conventions of speech (B1)

   The author uses dialogue to convey the theme or central idea in this story. The author does not use repetition, personification, or flashback in this story.

7.   Drawing conclusions (B2)

Sample answer: *Enrico is determined and hopeful. When Grandfather criticizes the short story Enrico has written, he is hurt and his pride is wounded, yet he tells Grandfather he will not give up. Grandfather says that writers need talent but also need great perseverance. Enrico seems to have both of these qualities.*

8.   Interpretations of the conventions of speech (B1)

Sample answer:

   The author included this detail to show that Grandfather was very intelligent and had a great deal of experience writing. This makes him an authority on the subject and experienced enough to guide Enrico in the right direction. This relates to the central idea of the story because Enrico wants to be a writer and turns to Grandfather for guidance.

Viewing
(Standard 3.5)

Developing the skill of viewing media is an important part of Language Arts literacy. Unfortunately, it does not get the attention it needs. Participating in viewing exercises will help you to review these skills: (A.1, 1.2, B.4, C.2).

When viewing a video text you will want to:

- recognize a theme or central idea.

- recognize details that develop the theme or central idea.

- recognize the organizational structure of the text.

- paraphrase, retell, or interpret what you see.

- determine purpose (entertain, persuade, or inform).

- make judgments, form opinions, and draw conclusions from the text.

- analyze use of the elements and conventions (humor, irony, setting, metaphor) that contribute to meaning.

- analyze how you feel about the text.

- interpret conventions of visual media.

During this year, you might be asked to view a video and answer questions about it. It is likely that you will see the video only once and you will not be able to take notes. Try to concentrate on the following points when watching the video, as these are commonly asked questions:

- What is the name of the video?

- What is the purpose of the video? Does it entertain, persuade, or provide information?

- What is the video mostly about?

- What are some of the main points in the video?

- What techniques did the creators use in the video? Did they use flashbacks? Suspense? Humor? Irony?

- Was the video effective?

ANSWER SHEETS

PRETEST and POSTTEST

Part 1—Explanatory Writing Task

_____

_____

_____

_____

_____

_____

_____

_____

_____

_____

_____

_____

_____

_____

_____

_____

_____

_____

_____

_____

_____

_____

_____

_____

_____

_____

_____

_____

_____

_____

_____

_____

_____

_____

_____

_____

_____

_____

_____

_____

_____

_____

_____

_____

_____

_____

_____

END OF PART 1—DO NOT GO ON TO THE NEXT PAGE.

Part 2—Multiple-Choice Section

1. Ⓐ Ⓑ Ⓒ Ⓓ

2. Ⓐ Ⓑ Ⓒ Ⓓ

3. Ⓐ Ⓑ Ⓒ Ⓓ

4. Ⓐ Ⓑ Ⓒ Ⓓ

5. Ⓐ Ⓑ Ⓒ Ⓓ

6. Ⓐ Ⓑ Ⓒ Ⓓ

7. Ⓐ Ⓑ Ⓒ Ⓓ

8. Ⓐ Ⓑ Ⓒ Ⓓ

9. Ⓐ Ⓑ Ⓒ Ⓓ

Part 2—Reading Open-Ended Response

10. _____

_____

_____

_____

_____

_____

_____

_____

_____

_____

_____

_____

_____

_____

_____

_____

_____

_____

_____

_____

_____

_____

Part 2—Reading Open-Ended Response

11. _____

_____

_____

_____

_____

_____

_____

_____

_____

_____

_____

_____

_____

_____

_____

_____

_____

_____

_____

_____

_____

_____

_____

_____

_____

Part 3—Multiple-Choice Section

12. (A) (B) (C) (D)

13. (A) (B) (C) (D)

14. (A) (B) (C) (D)

15. (A) (B) (C) (D)

16. (A) (B) (C) (D)

17. (A) (B) (C) (D)

18. (A) (B) (C) (D)

19. (A) (B) (C) (D)

20. (A) (B) (C) (D)

21. (A) (B) (C) (D)

22. (A) (B) (C) (D)

23. (A) (B) (C) (D)

24. (A) (B) (C) (D)

25. (A) (B) (C) (D)

Part 3—Reading Open-Ended Response

26. _____

_____

_____

_____

_____

_____

_____

_____

_____

_____

_____

_____

_____

_____

_____

_____

_____

_____

_____

_____

_____

Part 3—Reading Open-Ended Response

27. _____

_____

_____

_____

_____

_____

_____

_____

_____

_____

_____

_____

_____

_____

_____

_____

_____

_____

_____

_____

_____

END OF PART 3—DO NOT GO ON TO THE NEXT PAGE.

Part 4—Persuasive Writing Task

_____

_____

_____

_____

_____

_____

_____

_____

_____

_____

_____

_____

_____

_____

_____

_____

_____

_____

_____

_____

_____

_____

_____

_____

_____

_____

_____

_____

_____

_____

_____

_____

_____

_____

_____

_____

_____

_____

_____

_____

_____

_____

_____

_____

_____

_____

END OF PART 4

Part 1—Writing to Speculate Task A

_____

_____

_____

_____

_____

_____

_____

_____

_____

_____

_____

_____

_____

_____

_____

_____

_____

_____

_____

_____

_____

_____

_____

Part 2—Multiple-Choice Section

1. Ⓐ Ⓑ Ⓒ Ⓓ

2. Ⓐ Ⓑ Ⓒ Ⓓ

3. Ⓐ Ⓑ Ⓒ Ⓓ

4. Ⓐ Ⓑ Ⓒ Ⓓ

5. Ⓐ Ⓑ Ⓒ Ⓓ

6. Ⓐ Ⓑ Ⓒ Ⓓ

7. Ⓐ Ⓑ Ⓒ Ⓓ

8. Ⓐ Ⓑ Ⓒ Ⓓ

9. Ⓐ Ⓑ Ⓒ Ⓓ

Part 1—Reading Open-Ended Response

10. _____

_____

_____

_____

_____

_____

_____

_____

_____

_____

_____

_____

_____

_____

_____

_____

_____

_____

_____

_____

_____

_____

_____

END OF PART 1—DO NOT GO ON TO THE NEXT PAGE.

Part 3—Multiple-Choice Section

11. Ⓐ Ⓑ Ⓒ Ⓓ

12. Ⓐ Ⓑ Ⓒ Ⓓ

13. Ⓐ Ⓑ Ⓒ Ⓓ

14. Ⓐ Ⓑ Ⓒ Ⓓ

15. Ⓐ Ⓑ Ⓒ Ⓓ

16. Ⓐ Ⓑ Ⓒ Ⓓ

17. Ⓐ Ⓑ Ⓒ Ⓓ

18. Ⓐ Ⓑ Ⓒ Ⓓ

19. Ⓐ Ⓑ Ⓒ Ⓓ

20. Ⓐ Ⓑ Ⓒ Ⓓ

Part 3—Reading Open-Ended Response

21. _____

_____

_____

_____

_____

_____

_____

_____

_____

_____

_____

_____

_____

_____

_____

_____

_____

_____

_____

_____

_____

_____

_____

_____

_____

_____

_____

_____

END OF PART 3—DO NOT GO ON TO THE NEXT PAGE.

Part 4—Multiple-Choice Section

22. Ⓐ   Ⓑ   Ⓒ   Ⓓ

23. Ⓐ   Ⓑ   Ⓒ   Ⓓ

24. Ⓐ   Ⓑ   Ⓒ   Ⓓ

25. Ⓐ   Ⓑ   Ⓒ   Ⓓ

26. Ⓐ   Ⓑ   Ⓒ   Ⓓ

27. Ⓐ   Ⓑ   Ⓒ   Ⓓ

28. Ⓐ   Ⓑ   Ⓒ   Ⓓ

29. Ⓐ   Ⓑ   Ⓒ   Ⓓ

30. Ⓐ   Ⓑ   Ⓒ   Ⓓ

31. Ⓐ   Ⓑ   Ⓒ   Ⓓ

32. Ⓐ   Ⓑ   Ⓒ   Ⓓ

Part 4—Reading Open-Ended Response

33. _____

_____

_____

_____

_____

_____

_____

_____

_____

_____

_____

_____

_____

_____

_____

_____

_____

_____

_____

_____

_____

_____

_____

_____

Part 5—Writing to Persuade Task B

_____

_____

_____

_____

_____

_____

_____

_____

_____

_____

_____

_____

_____

_____

_____

_____

_____

_____

_____

_____

_____

_____

_____

_____

_____

_____

_____

_____

_____

_____

_____

_____

_____

_____

_____

_____

_____

_____

_____

_____

_____

_____

_____

_____

_____

_____

_____

_____

_____

_____

END OF PART 5—DO NOT GO ON TO THE NEXT PAGE.

Part 6—Multiple-Choice Section

35. Ⓐ Ⓑ Ⓒ Ⓓ

36. Ⓐ Ⓑ Ⓒ Ⓓ

37. Ⓐ Ⓑ Ⓒ Ⓓ

38. Ⓐ Ⓑ Ⓒ Ⓓ

39. Ⓐ Ⓑ Ⓒ Ⓓ

40. Ⓐ Ⓑ Ⓒ Ⓓ

41. Ⓐ Ⓑ Ⓒ Ⓓ

42. Ⓐ Ⓑ Ⓒ Ⓓ

Part 6—Reading Open-Ended Response

43. _____

_____

_____

_____

_____

_____

_____

_____

_____

_____

_____

_____

_____

_____

_____

_____

_____

_____

_____

END OF PART 6—DO NOT GO ON TO THE NEXT PAGE.

Speaking

_____
_____
_____
_____
_____
_____
_____
_____
_____
_____
_____
_____
_____
_____
_____
_____
_____
_____
_____
_____
_____

NOTES

NOTES

NOTES